Especially For

....

From

....

Date

....

One Thousand Promises

A Bible Promise Book® Journal

BARBOUR BOOKS
An Imprint of Barbour Publishing, Inc.

© 2018 by Barbour Publishing, Inc.

Written and compiled by Shanna D. Gregor.

Print ISBN 978-1-68322-598-0

All scripture quotations are taken from the King James Version of the Bible.

Published by Barbour Books, an imprint of Barbour Publishing, Inc., 1810 Barbour Drive, Uhrichsville, Ohio 44683, www.barbourbooks.com

Our mission is to inspire the world with the life-changing message of the Bible.

Member of the
Evangelical Christian
Publishers Association

Printed in China.

What do one thousand promises look like?
A life lived as God intended!
A life overflowing in love and gratitude!

This beautifully inspiring journal features a list of one thousand promises from God's Word—from the beloved King James Version—plus thought-provoking journal prompts that will encourage you to record your innermost thoughts and feelings about the One who loves you most.

One Thousand Promises will encourage you to live an extraordinary life filled with wonder at the many ways our Creator chooses to love, encourage, and bless your heart through His Word.

1. *For whatsoever is born of God overcometh the world: and this is the victory that overcometh the world, even our faith.* — 1 JOHN 5:4

2. *Trust in the LORD with all thine heart; and lean not unto thine own understanding. In all thy ways acknowledge him, and he shall direct thy paths.* — PROVERBS 3:5–6

3. *For by grace are ye saved through faith; and that not of yourselves: it is the gift of God: Not of works, lest any man should boast.* — EPHESIANS 2:8–9

My faith grows stronger when I. . .

....

....

....

....

....

....

....

....

....

....

....

....

....

....

....

4. *A soft answer turneth away wrath: but grievous words stir up anger.*
—PROVERBS 15:1

5. *The discretion of a man deferreth his anger; and it is his glory to pass over a transgression.* — PROVERBS 19:11

6. *Be ye angry, and sin not: let not the sun go down upon your wrath.* — EPHESIANS 4:26

I best manage my anger by...

....

....

....

....

....

....

....

....

....

....

....

....

....

....

....

....

7. The LORD is good unto them that wait for him, to the soul that seeketh him. —LAMENTATIONS 3:25

8. That they should seek the Lord, if haply they might feel after him, and find him, though he be not far from every one of us. — ACTS 17:27

9. Sow to yourselves in righteousness, reap in mercy; break up your fallow ground: for it is time to seek the LORD, till he come and rain righteousness upon you. — HOSEA 10:12

I feel closest to God when. . .

....

....

....

....

....

....

....

....

....

....

....

....

....

....

....

....

....

10. *Call unto me, and I will answer thee, and show thee great and mighty things, which thou knowest not.* — JEREMIAH 33:3

11. *Be careful for nothing; but in every thing by prayer and supplication with thanksgiving let your requests be made known unto God. And the peace of God, which passeth all understanding, shall keep your hearts and minds through Christ Jesus.* — PHILIPPIANS 4:6–7

12. *The sacrifice of the wicked is an abomination to the LORD: but the prayer of the upright is his delight.* — PROVERBS 15:8

When I pray, I feel. . .

....

....

....

....

....

....

....

....

....

....

....

....

....

....

13. *All the earth shall worship thee, and shall sing unto thee; they shall sing to thy name.* — Psalm 66:4

14. *Exalt the Lord our God, and worship at his holy hill; for the Lord our God is holy.* — Psalm 99:9

15. *God is a Spirit: and they that worship him must worship him in spirit and in truth.* — John 4:24

I make time to worship each day by. . .

....

....

....

....

....

....

....

....

....

....

....

....

....

....

....

....

16. *Search the scriptures; for in them ye think ye have eternal life: and they are they which testify of me.* — JOHN 5:39

17. *And Jesus answering said unto them, Do ye not therefore err, because ye know not the scriptures, neither the power of God?* — MARK 12:24

18. *So then faith cometh by hearing, and hearing by the word of God.* — ROMANS 10:17

It's important to spend time in God's Word because. . .

. . . .

. . . .

. . . .

. . . .

. . . .

. . . .

. . . .

. . . .

. . . .

. . . .

. . . .

. . . .

. . . .

. . . .

19. *As for God, his way is perfect; the word of the Lord is tried: he is a buckler to all them that trust in him.* — 2 Samuel 22:31

20. *Casting all your care upon him; for he careth for you.* — 1 Peter 5:7

21. *Blessed is that man that maketh the Lord his trust.* — Psalm 40:4

It's easiest for me to trust God when. . .

....

....

....

....

....

....

....

....

....

....

....

....

....

....

....

....

....

....

22. *And also that every man should eat and drink, and enjoy the good of all his labour, it is the gift of God.* — ECCLESIASTES 3:13

23. *In the house of the righteous is much treasure: but in the revenues of the wicked is trouble.* — PROVERBS 15:6

24. *But grow in grace, and in the knowledge of our Lord and Saviour Jesus Christ. To him be glory both now and for ever. Amen.* — 2 PETER 3:18

Some of God's best gifts in my life are...

....

....

....

....

....

....

....

....

....

....

....

....

....

....

25. *Ye shall know that I am the* LORD *your God.* — EXODUS 16:12

26. *Great is the* LORD, *and greatly to be praised; and his greatness is unsearchable.* — PSALM 145:3

27. *And they that know thy name will put their trust in thee: for thou,* LORD, *hast not forsaken them that seek thee.* — PSALM 9:10

When I make God the highest priority in my life...

28. *And they that are Christ's have crucified the flesh with the affections and lusts.* — GALATIANS 5:24

29. *Teaching us that, denying ungodliness and worldly lusts, we should live soberly, righteously, and godly, in this present world.* — TITUS 2:12

30. *Then said Jesus unto his disciples, If any man will come after me, let him deny himself, and take up his cross, and follow me.* — MATTHEW 16:24

When I choose God's way instead of my own. . .

31. *Therefore if any man be in Christ, he is a new creature: old things are passed away; behold, all things are become new.* — 2 CORINTHIANS 5:17

32. *For he hath made him to be sin for us, who knew no sin; that we might be made the righteousness of God in him.* — 2 CORINTHIANS 5:21

33. *And you, being dead in your sins and the uncircumcision of your flesh, hath he quickened together with him, having forgiven you all trespasses.* — COLOSSIANS 2:13

The gift of my salvation means so much to me because. . .

....

....

....

....

....

....

....

....

....

....

....

....

....

....

....

....

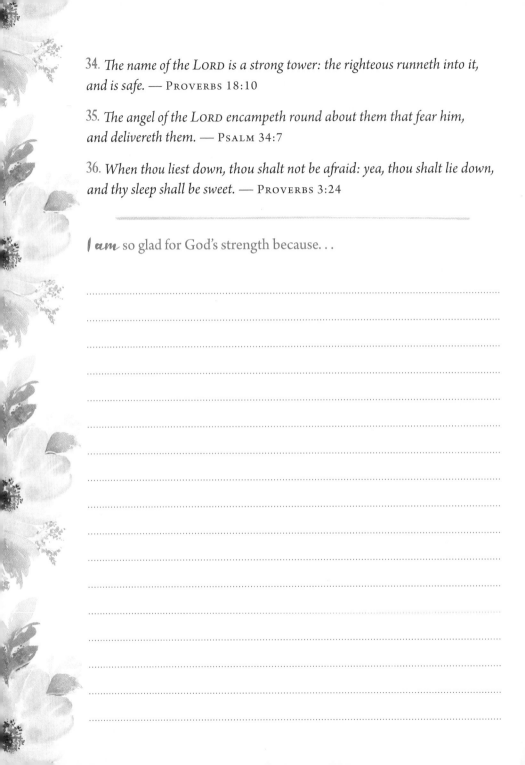

34. *The name of the* LORD *is a strong tower: the righteous runneth into it, and is safe.* — PROVERBS 18:10

35. *The angel of the* LORD *encampeth round about them that fear him, and delivereth them.* — PSALM 34:7

36. *When thou liest down, thou shalt not be afraid: yea, thou shalt lie down, and thy sleep shall be sweet.* — PROVERBS 3:24

I am so glad for God's strength because. . .

....

....

....

....

....

....

....

....

....

....

....

....

....

....

....

....

37. *Pride goeth before destruction, and a haughty spirit before a fall.*
— PROVERBS 16:18

38. *Let another man praise thee, and not thine own mouth; a stranger, and not thine own lips.* — PROVERBS 27:2

39. *An high look, and a proud heart, and the plowing of the wicked, is sin.*
— PROVERBS 21:4

When I give God all the credit, I feel. . .

40. *And all things, whatsoever ye shall ask in prayer, believing, ye shall receive.* — MATTHEW 21:22

41. *He will be very gracious unto thee at the voice of thy cry; when he shall hear it, he will answer thee.* — ISAIAH 30:19

42. *And it shall come to pass, that before they call, I will answer; and while they are yet speaking, I will hear.* — ISAIAH 65:24

When I pray, I know. . .

....

....

....

....

....

....

....

....

....

....

....

....

....

....

....

....

43. *Keep therefore the words of this covenant, and do them, that ye may prosper in all that ye do.* — DEUTERONOMY 29:9

44. *Those things, which ye have both learned, and received, and heard, and seen in me, do: and the God of peace shall be with you.* — PHILIPPIANS 4:9

45. *For not the hearers of the law are just before God, but the doers of the law shall be justified.* — ROMANS 2:13

I want to be obedient to God because. . .

46. *And he said, He that shewed mercy on him. Then said Jesus unto him, Go, and do thou likewise.* — Luke 10:37

47. *For my name's sake will I defer mine anger, and for my praise will I refrain for thee, that I cut thee not off.* — Isaiah 48:9

48. *For in my wrath I smote thee, but in my favour have I had mercy on thee.* — Isaiah 60:10

I am grateful for God's mercy because. . .

49. *A man that beareth false witness against his neighbour is a maul, and a sword, and a sharp arrow.* — PROVERBS 25:18

50. *A faithful witness will not lie: but a false witness will utter lies.* — PROVERBS 14:5

51. *But if ye have bitter envying and strife in your hearts, glory not, and lie not against the truth.* — JAMES 3:14

Speaking truth and honesty is so important because. . .

....

....

....

....

....

....

....

....

....

....

....

....

....

....

....

....

52. *For God so loved the world, that he gave his only begotten Son, that whosoever believeth in him should not perish, but have everlasting life.* — JOHN 3:16

53. *Herein is love, not that we loved God, but that he loved us, and sent his Son to be the propitiation for our sins.* — 1 JOHN 4:10

54. *I will heal their backsliding, I will love them freely: for mine anger is turned away from him.* — HOSEA 14:4

God's unconditional love has changed me in many ways. . .

....

....

....

....

....

....

....

....

....

....

....

....

....

....

....

....

55. *The voice of rejoicing and salvation is in the tabernacles of the righteous: the right hand of the LORD doeth valiantly.* — PSALM 118:15

56. *These things have I spoken unto you, that my joy might remain in you, and that your joy might be full.* — JOHN 15:11

57. *Yet I will rejoice in the LORD, I will joy in the God of my salvation.* — HABAKKUK 3:18

The joy of the Lord bubbles over within me when. . .

....

....

....

....

....

....

....

....

....

....

....

....

....

....

58. *Who by him do believe in God, that raised him up from the dead, and gave him glory; that your faith and hope might be in God.* — 1 Peter 1:21

59. *For the hope which is laid up for you in heaven, whereof ye heard before in the word of the truth of the gospel.* — Colossians 1:5

60. *Be of good courage, and he shall strengthen your heart, all ye that hope in the Lord.* — Psalm 31:24

God gives me hope because...

....
....
....
....
....
....
....
....
....
....
....
....
....
....
....
....
....

61. *But the salvation of the righteous is of the LORD: he is their strength in the time of trouble.* — PSALM 37:39

62. *The LORD is good, a strong hold in the day of trouble; and he knoweth them that trust in him.* — NAHUM 1:7

63. *Thou art my hiding place; thou shalt preserve me from trouble; thou shalt compass me about with songs of deliverance.* — PSALM 32:7

When trouble comes, I rely on God for. . .

64. *And thine ears shall hear a word behind thee, saying, This is the way, walk ye in it, when ye turn to the right hand, and when ye turn to the left.* — ISAIAH 30:21

65. *For this God is our God for ever and ever: he will be our guide even unto death.* — PSALM 48:14

66. *For his God doth instruct him to discretion, and doth teach him.* — ISAIAH 28:26

I trust the Lord to guide me in all ways, including. . .

67. *Thou shalt not go up and down as a talebearer among thy people: neither shalt thou stand against the blood of thy neighbour: I am the Lord.*
— Leviticus 19:16

68. *The words of a talebearer are as wounds, and they go down into the innermost parts of the belly.* — Proverbs 18:8

69. *The tongue deviseth mischiefs; like a sharp razor, working deceitfully.*
— Psalm 52:2

When I am tempted to gossip, God's Word reminds me. . .

....

....

....

....

....

....

....

....

....

....

....

....

....

....

....

70. *And when ye stand praying, forgive, if ye have ought against any: that your Father also which is in heaven may forgive you your trespasses.*
— MARK 11:25

71. *For if ye forgive men their trespasses, your heavenly Father will also forgive you.* — MATTHEW 6:14

72. *Be not overcome of evil, but overcome evil with good.* — ROMANS 12:21

When I am struggling with forgiveness, it's important for me to. . .

....

....

....

....

....

....

....

....

....

....

....

....

....

....

....

....

73. *Now faith is the substance of things hoped for, the evidence of things not seen.* — HEBREWS 11:1

74. *It is of the LORD's mercies that we are not consumed, because his compassions fail not. They are new every morning: great is thy faithfulness.* — LAMENTATIONS 3:22–23

75. *For ye are all the children of God by faith in Christ Jesus.* — GALATIANS 3:26

The things I am learning about my faith include. . .

....

....

....

....

....

....

....

....

....

....

....

....

....

....

....

76. *He giveth power to the faint; and to them that have no might he increaseth strength.* — Isaiah 40:29

77. *Trust in the Lord, and do good; so shalt thou dwell in the land, and verily thou shalt be fed.* — Psalm 37:3

78. *Fear not: for they that be with us are more than they that be with them.* — 2 Kings 6:16

I can overcome my fears because. . .

....

....

....

....

....

....

....

....

....

....

....

....

....

....

....

79. He that hath pity upon the poor lendeth unto the LORD; and that which he hath given will he pay him again. — PROVERBS 19:17

80. He that despiseth his neighbour sinneth: but he that hath mercy on the poor, happy is he. — PROVERBS 14:21

81. He hath dispersed, he hath given to the poor; his righteousness endureth for ever; his horn shall be exalted with honour. — PSALM 112:9

I open my heart and hands to those in need by. . .

82. *And they said, Believe on the Lord Jesus Christ, and thou shalt be saved, and thy house.* — ACTS 16:31

83. *I am come a light into the world, that whosoever believeth on me should not abide in darkness.* — JOHN 12:46

84. *Jesus said unto him, If thou canst believe, all things are possible to him that believeth.* — MARK 9:23

When I am tempted to doubt, I like to think about. . .

85. *A sound heart is the life of the flesh: but envy the rottenness of the bones.* — PROVERBS 14:30

86. *But godliness with contentment is great gain.* — 1 TIMOTHY 6:6

87. *A merry heart doeth good like a medicine: but a broken spirit drieth the bones.* — PROVERBS 17:22

I find contentment in. . .

....

....

....

....

....

....

....

....

....

....

....

....

....

....

....

....

....

....

....

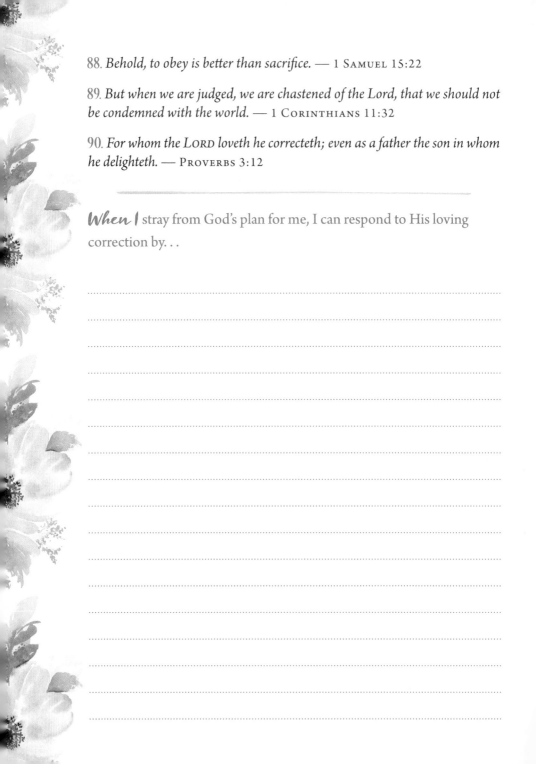

88. *Behold, to obey is better than sacrifice.* — 1 Samuel 15:22

89. *But when we are judged, we are chastened of the Lord, that we should not be condemned with the world.* — 1 Corinthians 11:32

90. *For whom the Lord loveth he correcteth; even as a father the son in whom he delighteth.* — Proverbs 3:12

When I stray from God's plan for me, I can respond to His loving correction by. . .

91. *His heart is established, he shall not be afraid, until he see his desire upon his enemies.* — PSALM 112:8

92. *No weapon that is formed against thee shall prosper; and every tongue that shall rise against thee in judgment thou shalt condemn.* — ISAIAH 54:17

93. *When a man's ways please the LORD, he maketh even his enemies to be at peace with him.* — PROVERBS 16:7

It's hard to love my enemies, but God's Word reminds me. . .

....

....

....

....

....

....

....

....

....

....

....

....

....

....

....

....

94. *For the wages of sin is death; but the gift of God is eternal life through Jesus Christ our Lord.* — ROMANS 6:23

95. *For he that soweth to his flesh shall of the flesh reap corruption; but he that soweth to the Spirit shall of the Spirit reap life everlasting.* — GALATIANS 6:8

96. *For we know that if our earthly house of this tabernacle were dissolved, we have a building of God, an house not made with hands, eternal in the heavens.* — 2 CORINTHIANS 5:1

The promise of eternal life gives me hope because. . .

....
....
....
....
....
....
....
....
....
....
....
....
....
....
....
....
....

97. *(For the* LORD *thy God is a merciful God;) he will not forsake thee, neither destroy thee, nor forget the covenant of thy fathers which he sware unto them.* — DEUTERONOMY 4:31

98. *He hath remembered his covenant for ever, the word which he commanded to a thousand generations.* — PSALM 105:8

99. *Let us hold fast the profession of our faith without wavering; (for he is faithful that promised).* — HEBREWS 10:23

God's promise never to leave me nor forsake me helps me to. . .

....

....

....

....

....

....

....

....

....

....

....

....

....

....

....

100. *For I the LORD thy God will hold thy right hand, saying unto thee, Fear not; I will help thee.* — ISAIAH 41:13

101. *But whoso hearkeneth unto me shall dwell safely, and shall be quiet from fear of evil.* — PROVERBS 1:33

102. *For God hath not given us the spirit of fear; but of power, and of love, and of a sound mind.* — 2 TIMOTHY 1:7

The fears I daily give to God include. . .

....
....
....
....
....
....
....
....
....
....
....
....
....
....
....
....

103. *I will abundantly bless her provision: I will satisfy her poor with bread.* — PSALM 132:15

104. *But my God shall supply all your need according to his riches in glory by Christ Jesus.* — PHILIPPIANS 4:19

105. *Delight thyself also in the LORD: and he shall give thee the desires of thine heart.* — PSALM 37:4

I know I can rely on God to provide what I need because...

....

....

....

....

....

....

....

....

....

....

....

....

....

....

....

....

106. *I will be as the dew unto Israel: he shall grow as the lily, and cast forth his roots as Lebanon.* — HOSEA 14:5

107. *For if these things be in you, and abound, they make you that ye shall neither be barren nor unfruitful in the knowledge of our Lord Jesus Christ.* — 2 PETER 1:8

108. *Every branch in me that beareth not fruit he taketh away: and every branch that beareth fruit, he purgeth it, that it may bring forth more fruit.* — JOHN 15:2

Things that help me stay rooted in my faith include...

....
....
....
....
....
....
....
....
....
....
....
....
....
....
....
....
....
....

109. *If we confess our sins, he is faithful and just to forgive us our sins, and to cleanse us from all unrighteousness.* — 1 JOHN 1:9

110. *As far as the east is from the west, so far hath he removed our transgressions from us.* — PSALM 103:12

111. *For the LORD your God is gracious and merciful, and will not turn away his face from you, if ye return unto him.* — 2 CHRONICLES 30:9

I never have to feel guilty because. . .

112. *I will not leave you comfortless: I will come to you.* — JOHN 14:18

113. *Then shalt thou call, and the LORD shall answer; thou shalt cry, and he shall say, Here I am.* — ISAIAH 58:9

114. *And will be a Father unto you, and ye shall be my sons and daughters, saith the Lord Almighty.* — 2 CORINTHIANS 6:18

When I feel alone, this is my prayer to God. . .

115. *A good man sheweth favour, and lendeth: he will guide his affairs with discretion.* — PSALM 112:5

116. *Give, and it shall be given unto you; good measure, pressed down, and shaken together, and running over, shall men give into your bosom.* — LUKE 6:38

117. *The liberal soul shall be made fat: and he that watereth shall be watered also himself.* — PROVERBS 11:25

When I give to others, it blesses me most because. . .

....

....

....

....

....

....

....

....

....

....

....

....

....

....

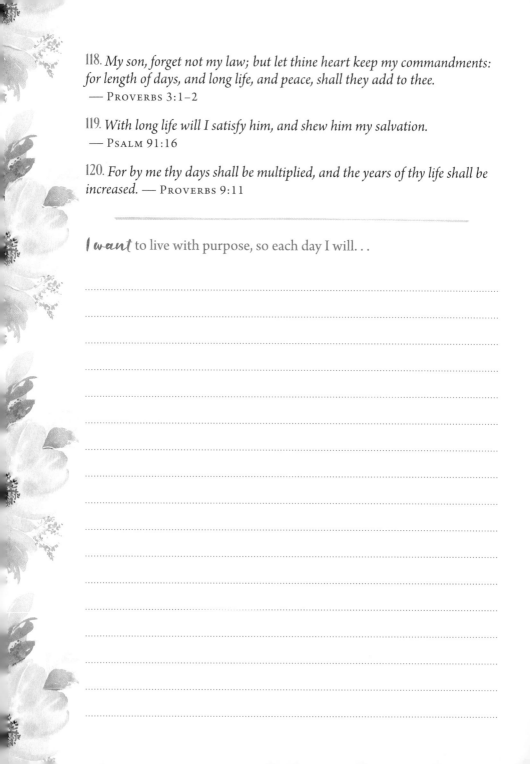

118. *My son, forget not my law; but let thine heart keep my commandments: for length of days, and long life, and peace, shall they add to thee.*
— PROVERBS 3:1–2

119. *With long life will I satisfy him, and shew him my salvation.*
— PSALM 91:16

120. *For by me thy days shall be multiplied, and the years of thy life shall be increased.* — PROVERBS 9:11

I want to live with purpose, so each day I will. . .

121. *We love him, because he first loved us.* — 1 JOHN 4:19

122. *God is love; and he that dwelleth in love dwelleth in God, and God in him.* — 1 JOHN 4:16

123. *The way of the wicked is an abomination unto the LORD: but he loveth him that followeth after righteousness.* — PROVERBS 15:9

Because of God's unfailing love. . .

....

....

....

....

....

....

....

....

....

....

....

....

....

....

....

....

....

124. *Blessed are the meek: for they shall inherit the earth.* — MATTHEW 5:5

125. *The LORD lifteth up the meek: he casteth the wicked down to the ground.* — PSALM 147:6

126. *Put them in mind to be subject to principalities and powers, to obey magistrates, to be ready to every good work, to speak evil of no man, to be no brawlers, but gentle, shewing all meekness unto all men.* — TITUS 3:1–2

When I respond in gentleness to others. . .

127. *And let us not be weary in well doing: for in due season we shall reap, if we faint not.* — GALATIANS 6:9

128. *And now, Lord, what wait I for? my hope is in thee.* — PSALM 39:7

129. *For ye have need of patience, that, after ye have done the will of God, ye might receive the promise.* — HEBREWS 10:36

Waiting is often hard, but God's timing is. . .

130. *Now the Lord of peace himself give you peace always by all means.*
— 2 Thessalonians 3:16

131. *And the peace of God, which passeth all understanding, shall keep your hearts and minds through Christ Jesus.* — Philippians 4:7

132. *And the work of righteousness shall be peace; and the effect of righteousness quietness and assurance for ever.* — Isaiah 32:17

When my mind is filled with overwhelming thoughts, God's peace is...

....

....

....

....

....

....

....

....

....

....

....

....

....

....

133. *He shall call upon me, and I will answer him.* — PSALM 91:15

134. *And I say unto you, Ask, and it shall be given you; seek, and ye shall find; knock, and it shall be opened unto you.* — LUKE 11:9

135. *The Lord is far from the wicked: but he heareth the prayer of the righteous.* — PROVERBS 15:29

Prayer changes me because. . .

....

....

....

....

....

....

....

....

....

....

....

....

....

....

136. *For I will restore health unto thee, and I will heal thee of thy wounds, saith the LORD.* — JEREMIAH 30:17

137. *Beloved, I wish above all things that thou mayest prosper and be in health, even as thy soul prospereth.* — 3 JOHN 2

138. *Heal me, O Lord, and I shall be healed; save me, and I shall be saved: for thou art my praise.* — JEREMIAH 17:14

I believe God can bring healing in my life because. . .

....

....

....

....

....

....

....

....

....

....

....

....

....

....

....

....

139. *A new spirit will I put within you: and I will take away the stony heart out of your flesh, and I will give you an heart of flesh.* — EZEKIEL 36:26

140. *To him give all the prophets witness, that through his name whosoever believeth in him shall receive remission of sins.* — ACTS 10:43

141. *For thou, Lord, art good, and ready to forgive; and plenteous in mercy unto all them that call upon thee.* — PSALM 86:5

When I struggle to forgive myself. . .

....

....

....

....

....

....

....

....

....

....

....

....

....

....

....

....

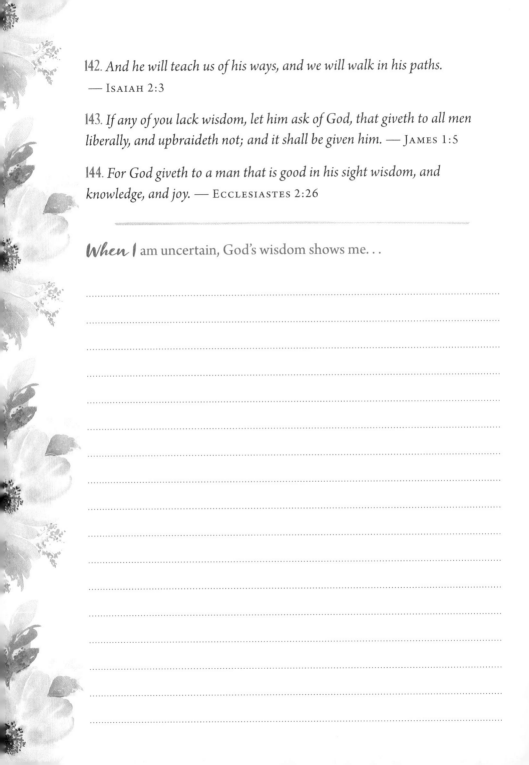

142. *And he will teach us of his ways, and we will walk in his paths.* — ISAIAH 2:3

143. *If any of you lack wisdom, let him ask of God, that giveth to all men liberally, and upbraideth not; and it shall be given him.* — JAMES 1:5

144. *For God giveth to a man that is good in his sight wisdom, and knowledge, and joy.* — ECCLESIASTES 2:26

When I am uncertain, God's wisdom shows me. . .

145. *For I am not ashamed of the gospel of Christ: for it is the power of God unto salvation to every one that believeth.* — ROMANS 1:16

146. *The entrance of thy words giveth light; it giveth understanding unto the simple.* — PSALM 119:130

147. *Blessed is he that readeth, and they that hear the words of this prophecy, and keep those things which are written therein: for the time is at hand.* — REVELATION 1:3

I better understand God's Word when I. . .

....

....

....

....

....

....

....

....

....

....

....

....

....

....

....

....

148. *And in every work that he began in the service of the house of God, and in the law, and in the commandments, to seek his God, he did it with all his heart, and prospered.* — 2 CHRONICLES 31:21

149. *Come unto me, all ye that labour and are heavy laden, and I will give you rest.* — MATTHEW 11:28

150. *That ye might walk worthy of the Lord unto all pleasing, being fruitful in every good work, and increasing in the knowledge of God.* — COLOSSIANS 1:10

My work can be frustrating, but I can always find joy in it by. . .

....

....

....

....

....

....

....

....

....

....

....

....

....

....

....

....

151. *For they all saw him, and were troubled. And immediately he talked with them, and saith unto them, Be of good cheer: it is I; be not afraid.*
— MARK 6:50

152. *Let not your heart be troubled: ye believe in God, believe also in me.*
— JOHN 14:1

153. *We are troubled on every side, yet not distressed; we are perplexed, but not in despair; persecuted, but not forsaken; cast down, but not destroyed.*
— 2 CORINTHIANS 4:8–9

Whenever I worry, I try to remember. . .

....

....

....

....

....

....

....

....

....

....

....

....

....

....

154. *For thou shalt worship no other god: for the* LORD, *whose name is Jealous, is a jealous God.* — EXODUS 34:14

155. *I will praise the* LORD *according to his righteousness: and will sing praise to the name of the* LORD *most high.* — PSALM 7:17

156. *And Jesus answered and said unto him, Get thee behind me, Satan: for it is written, Thou shalt worship the Lord thy God, and him only shalt thou serve.* — LUKE 4:8

To me, worship is. . .

....

....

....

....

....

....

....

....

....

....

....

....

....

....

....

157. *Hearken unto me, ye that know righteousness, the people in whose heart is my law; fear ye not the reproach of men, neither be ye afraid of their revilings.* — ISAIAH 51:7

158. *Thou shalt hide them in the secret of thy presence from the pride of man: thou shalt keep them secretly in a pavilion from the strife of tongues.* — PSALM 31:20

159. *And ye shall be hated of all men for my name's sake: but he that endureth to the end shall be saved.* — MATTHEW 10:22

I don't need to let the opinions of others weigh on me because. . .

....

....

....

....

....

....

....

....

....

....

....

....

....

....

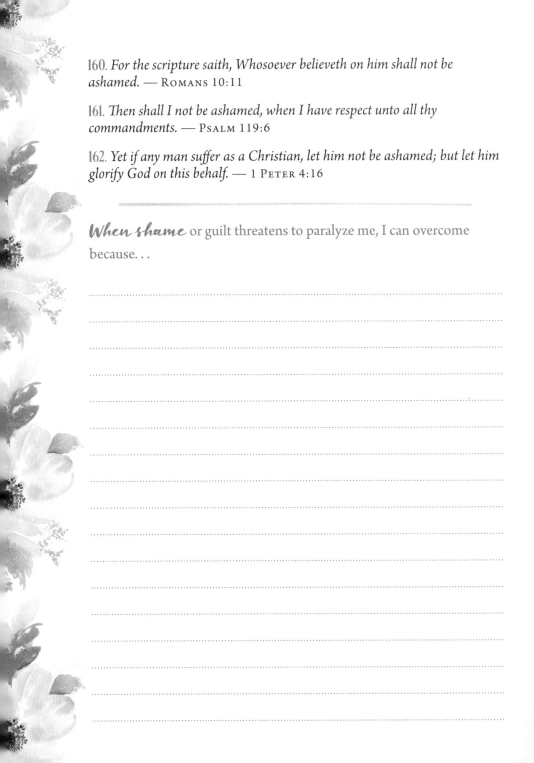

160. *For the scripture saith, Whosoever believeth on him shall not be ashamed.* — Romans 10:11

161. *Then shall I not be ashamed, when I have respect unto all thy commandments.* — Psalm 119:6

162. *Yet if any man suffer as a Christian, let him not be ashamed; but let him glorify God on this behalf.* — 1 Peter 4:16

When shame or guilt threatens to paralyze me, I can overcome because. . .

....

....

....

....

....

....

....

....

....

....

....

....

....

....

....

163. *The way of a fool is right in his own eyes: but he that hearkeneth unto counsel is wise.* — PROVERBS 12:15

164. *For if a man think himself to be something, when he is nothing, he deceiveth himself.* — GALATIANS 6:3

165. *Jesus said unto them, If ye were blind, ye should have no sin: but now ye say, We see; therefore your sin remaineth.* — JOHN 9:41

My prayer for humility is this. . .

....

....

....

....

....

....

....

....

....

....

....

....

....

....

166. *For what is a man profited, if he shall gain the whole world, and lose his own soul? or what shall a man give in exchange for his soul?* — MATTHEW 16:26

167. *For even Christ pleased not himself; but, as it is written, The reproaches of them that reproached thee fell on me.* — ROMANS 15:3

168. *For do I now persuade men, or God? or do I seek to please men? for if I yet pleased men, I should not be the servant of Christ.* — GALATIANS 1:10

If I work to please others instead of Christ. . .

169. *Even to them that believe on his name: which were born, not of blood, nor of the will of the flesh, nor of the will of man, but of God.* — JOHN 1:12–13

170. *Being born again, not of corruptible seed, but of incorruptible, by the word of God, which liveth and abideth for ever.* — 1 PETER 1:23

171. *Beloved, let us love one another: for love is of God; and every one that loveth is born of God, and knoweth God.* — 1 JOHN 4:7

When I feel like I don't belong, my heavenly Father reminds me that. . .

....

....

....

....

....

....

....

....

....

....

....

....

....

....

....

....

172. *For the LORD God is a sun and shield: the LORD will give grace and glory: no good thing will he withhold from them that walk uprightly.*
— PSALM 84:11

173. *The young lions do lack, and suffer hunger: but they that seek the LORD shall not want any good thing.* — PSALM 34:10

174. *He that spared not his own Son, but delivered him up for us all, how shall he not with him also freely give us all things?* — ROMANS 8:32

God's grace is always enough because. . .

....

....

....

....

....

....

....

....

....

....

....

....

....

....

....

....

....

175. The LORD is nigh unto them that are of a broken heart; and saveth such as be of a contrite spirit. — PSALM 34:18

176. The time is fulfilled, and the kingdom of God is at hand: repent ye, and believe the gospel. — MARK 1:15

177. Repent ye therefore, and be converted, that your sins may be blotted out, when the times of refreshing shall come from the presence of the Lord. — ACTS 3:19

When I confess my mistakes. . .

....

....

....

....

....

....

....

....

....

....

....

....

....

....

....

....

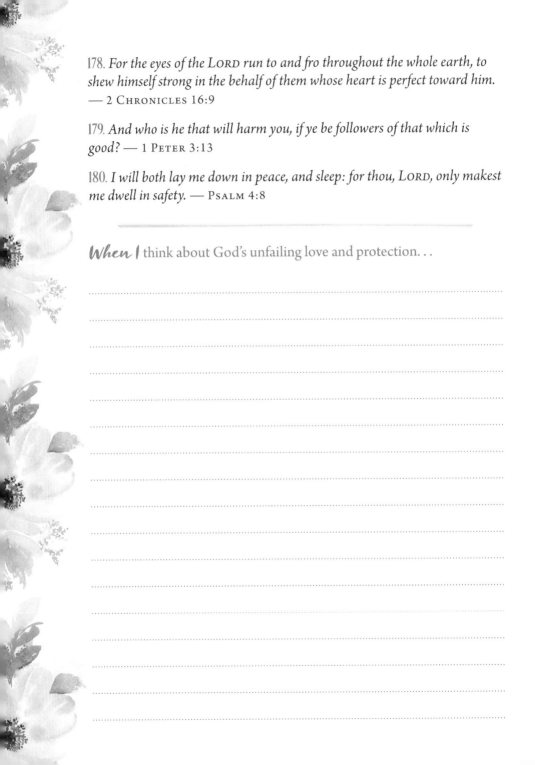

178. *For the eyes of the L*ORD *run to and fro throughout the whole earth, to shew himself strong in the behalf of them whose heart is perfect toward him.*
— 2 CHRONICLES 16:9

179. *And who is he that will harm you, if ye be followers of that which is good?* — 1 PETER 3:13

180. *I will both lay me down in peace, and sleep: for thou, L*ORD, *only makest me dwell in safety.* — PSALM 4:8

When I think about God's unfailing love and protection. . .

181. *Wherefore, my beloved brethren, let every man be swift to hear, slow to speak, slow to wrath: for the wrath of man worketh not the righteousness of God.* — JAMES 1:19–20

182. *The LORD is gracious, and full of compassion; slow to anger, and of great mercy.* — PSALM 145:8

183. *Be not hasty in thy spirit to be angry: for anger resteth in the bosom of fools.* — ECCLESIASTES 7:9

When I am tempted to let my emotions rule, my prayer is this. . .

184. *Jesus saith unto him, Thomas, because thou hast seen me, thou hast believed: blessed are they that have not seen, and yet have believed.*
— JOHN 20:29

185. *He that believeth on the Son hath everlasting life: and he that believeth not the Son shall not see life; but the wrath of God abideth on him.*
— JOHN 3:36

186. *And seek not ye what ye shall eat, or what ye shall drink, neither be ye of doubtful mind.* — LUKE 12:29

In times of doubt, God's Word reminds me. . .

....

....

....

....

....

....

....

....

....

....

....

....

....

....

187. *Give, and it shall be given unto you; good measure, pressed down, and shaken together, and running over, shall men give into your bosom.*
— LUKE 6:38

188. *But who am I, and what is my people, that we should be able to offer so willingly after this sort? for all things come of thee, and of thine own have we given thee.* — 1 CHRONICLES 29:14

189. *For every beast of the forest is mine, and the cattle upon a thousand hills. I know all the fowls of the mountains: and the wild beasts of the field are mine.* — PSALM 50:10–11

When I am tempted to hold tightly to things of the world, I. . .

....

....

....

....

....

....

....

....

....

....

....

....

....

190. *In the multitude of my thoughts within me thy comforts delight my soul.* — Psalm 94:19

191. *Though he fall, he shall not be utterly cast down: for the Lord upholdeth him with his hand.* — Psalm 37:24

192. *This is my comfort in my affliction: for thy word hath quickened me.* — Psalm 119:50

When Jesus envelops me in His comfort, I feel. . .

193. *Behold, the heaven and the heaven of heavens is the* LORD'S *thy God, the earth also, with all that therein is.* — DEUTERONOMY 10:14

194. *O* LORD, *how manifold are thy works! in wisdom hast thou made them all: the earth is full of thy riches.* — PSALM 104:24

195. *But thou shalt remember the* LORD *thy God: for it is he that giveth thee power to get wealth, that he may establish his covenant which he sware unto thy fathers, as it is this day.* — DEUTERONOMY 8:18

It helps me to remember everything belongs to God because. . .

....

....

....

....

....

....

....

....

....

....

....

....

....

....

196. *And all thy children shall be taught of the LORD; and great shall be the peace of thy children.* — Isaiah 54:13

197. *For I will pour water upon him that is thirsty, and floods upon the dry ground: I will pour my spirit upon thy seed, and my blessing upon thine offspring.* — Isaiah 44:3

198. *For the promise is unto you, and to your children, and to all that are afar off, even as many as the LORD our God shall call.* — Acts 2:39

I am thankful for the children God has placed in my life, because. . .

....

....

....

....

....

....

....

....

....

....

....

....

....

....

....

....

199. *So that we may boldly say, The Lord is my helper, and I will not fear what man shall do unto me.* — HEBREWS 13:6

200. *That we should be saved from our enemies, and from the hand of all that hate us.* — LUKE 1:71

201. *For I am with thee, and no man shall set on thee to hurt thee: for I have much people in this city.* — ACTS 18:10

When others oppose me, I . . .

202. *Fear not, little flock; for it is your Father's good pleasure to give you the kingdom.* — LUKE 12:32

203. *And he said unto them, Why are ye so fearful? how is it that ye have no faith?* — MARK 4:40

204. *The LORD shall give thee rest from thy sorrow, and from thy fear, and from the hard bondage wherein thou wast made to serve.* — ISAIAH 14:3

My faith should be bigger than my fears because. . .

....

....

....

....

....

....

....

....

....

....

....

....

....

....

205. *A God ready to pardon, gracious and merciful, slow to anger, and of great kindness. . .* — NEHEMIAH 9:17

206. *For his anger endureth but a moment; in his favour is life: weeping may endure for a night, but joy cometh in the morning.* — PSALM 30:5

207. *Draw nigh to God, and he will draw nigh to you. Cleanse your hands, ye sinners; and purify your hearts, ye double minded.* — JAMES 4:8

I feel farthest from God when. . .

208. *Therefore take no thought, saying, What shall we eat? or, What shall we drink? or, Wherewithal shall we be clothed? . . . for your heavenly Father knoweth that ye have need of all these things.* — MATTHEW 6:31–32

209. *And ye shall eat in plenty, and be satisfied, and praise the name of the LORD your God, that hath dealt wondrously with you: and my people shall never be ashamed.* — JOEL 2:26

210. *He hath given meat unto them that fear him: he will ever be mindful of his covenant.* — PSALM 111:5

I trust God because. . .

....

....

....

....

....

....

....

....

....

....

....

....

....

....

211. *The LORD will perfect that which concerneth me: thy mercy, O LORD, endureth for ever: forsake not the works of thine own hands.* — PSALM 138:8

212. *Which is come unto you, as it is in all the world; and bringeth forth fruit, as it doth also in you, since the day ye heard of it, and knew the grace of God in truth.* — COLOSSIANS 1:6

213. *I press toward the mark for the prize of the high calling of God in Christ Jesus.* — PHILIPPIANS 3:14

I know I'm growing in God's grace when. . .

....

....

....

....

....

....

....

....

....

....

....

....

....

....

214. *I will make darkness light before them, and crooked things straight. These things will I do unto them, and not forsake them.* — Isaiah 42:16

215. *The steps of a good man are ordered by the Lord: and he delighteth in his way.* — Psalm 37:23

216. *In all thy ways acknowledge him, and he shall direct thy paths.* — Proverbs 3:6

I have full confidence in God's guidance because. . .

217. *Better is a little with righteousness than great revenues without right.*
— PROVERBS 16:8

218. *Ye shall not steal, neither deal falsely, neither lie one to another.*
— LEVITICUS 19:11

219. *A false balance is abomination to the LORD: but a just weight is his delight.* — PROVERBS 11:1

When I wrestle with honesty, I. . .

....

....

....

....

....

....

....

....

....

....

....

....

....

....

....

....

220. *Use hospitality one to another without grudging. As every man hath received the gift, even so minister the same one to another, as good stewards of the manifold grace of God.* — 1 PETER 4:9–10

221. *For whosoever shall give you a cup of water to drink in my name, because ye belong to Christ, verily I say unto you, he shall not lose his reward.* — MARK 9:41

222. *Be not forgetful to entertain strangers: for thereby some have entertained angels unawares.* — HEBREWS 13:2

When I open my heart and home to others. . .

....

....

....

....

....

....

....

....

....

....

....

....

....

....

....

223. *Humble yourselves therefore under the mighty hand of God, that he may exalt you in due time.* — 1 PETER 5:6

224. *A man's pride shall bring him low: but honour shall uphold the humble in spirit.* — PROVERBS 29:23

225. *The fear of the LORD is the instruction of wisdom; and before honour is humility.* — PROVERBS 15:33

Humility is important to me because. . .

....

....

....

....

....

....

....

....

....

....

....

....

....

....

226. *Cast me not off in the time of old age; forsake me not when my strength faileth.* — PSALM 71:9

227. *With the ancient is wisdom; and in length of days understanding. With him is wisdom and strength, he hath counsel and understanding.* — JOB 12:12–13

228. *And even to your old age I am he; and even to hoar hairs will I carry you: I have made, and I will bear; even I will carry, and will deliver you.* — ISAIAH 46:4

With the blessing of a long life comes. . .

....

....

....

....

....

....

....

....

....

....

....

....

....

....

229. *He that loveth his brother abideth in the light, and there is none occasion of stumbling in him.* — 1 John 2:10

230. *Seeing ye have purified your souls in obeying the truth through the Spirit unto unfeigned love of the brethren, see that ye love one another with a pure heart fervently.* — 1 Peter 1:22

231. *But as touching brotherly love ye need not that I write unto you: for ye yourselves are taught of God to love one another.* — 1 Thessalonians 4:9

When I choose to love others, I feel. . .

....

....

....

....

....

....

....

....

....

....

....

....

....

....

....

232. But as it is written, Eye hath not seen, nor ear heard, neither have entered into the heart of man, the things which God hath prepared for them that love him. — 1 Corinthians 2:9

233. Grace be with all them that love our Lord Jesus Christ in sincerity. Amen. — Ephesians 6:24

234. The Lord preserveth all them that love him: but all the wicked will he destroy. — Psalm 145:20

When I think about God's never-ending love for me, I feel. . .

....

....

....

....

....

....

....

....

....

....

....

....

....

....

....

....

235. He that hath no rule over his own spirit is like a city that is broken down, and without walls. — PROVERBS 25:28

236. Search me, O God, and know my heart: try me, and know my thoughts. — PSALM 139:23

237. Dearly beloved, I beseech you as strangers and pilgrims, abstain from fleshly lusts, which war against the soul. — 1 PETER 2:11

God gives me tools to help me keep my thoughts and desires under control, including. . .

238. *The lip of truth shall be established for ever: but a lying tongue is but for a moment.* — PROVERBS 12:19

239. *Thou shalt not raise a false report: put not thine hand with the wicked to be an unrighteous witness.* — EXODUS 23:1

240. *A false witness shall not be unpunished, and he that speaketh lies shall not escape.* — PROVERBS 19:5

When temptation seems too great a burden to bear, this is my prayer. . .

241. *Hatred stirreth up strifes: but love covereth all sins.* — PROVERBS 10:12

242. *A scorner loveth not one that reproveth him: neither will he go unto the wise.* — PROVERBS 15:12

243. *What doth the LORD require of thee, but to do justly, and to love mercy, and to walk humbly with thy God?* — MICAH 6:8

I can best love my difficult-to-love family members by. . .

244. *The meek also shall increase their joy in the LORD, and the poor among men shall rejoice in the Holy One of Israel.* — ISAIAH 29:19

245. *But with righteousness shall he judge the poor, and reprove with equity for the meek of the earth.* — ISAIAH 11:4

246. *Let it be the hidden man of the heart, in that which is not corruptible, even the ornament of a meek and quiet spirit, which is in the sight of God of great price.* — 1 PETER 3:4

My "joy in the Lord" increases when. . .

....

....

....

....

....

....

....

....

....

....

....

....

....

....

....

....

247. *And therefore will the* LORD *wait, that he may be gracious unto you. . . for the* LORD *is a God of judgment: blessed are all they that wait for him.*
— ISAIAH 30:18

248. *But the mercy of the* LORD *is from everlasting to everlasting upon them that fear him, and his righteousness unto children's children.*
— PSALM 103:17

249. *I will proclaim the name of the* LORD *before thee; and will be gracious to whom I will be gracious, and will shew mercy on whom I will shew mercy.*
— EXODUS 33:19

I should choose to show mercy to those who I feel are undeserving because. . .

....

....

....

....

....

....

....

....

....

....

....

....

....

....

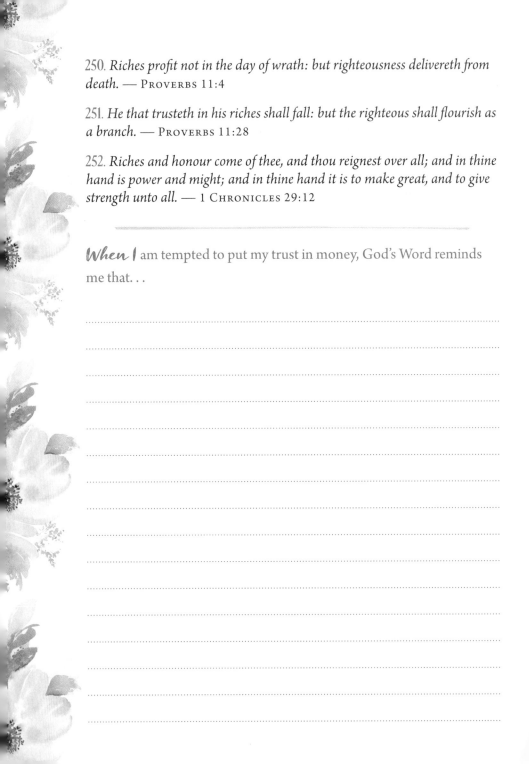

250. *Riches profit not in the day of wrath: but righteousness delivereth from death.* — PROVERBS 11:4

251. *He that trusteth in his riches shall fall: but the righteous shall flourish as a branch.* — PROVERBS 11:28

252. *Riches and honour come of thee, and thou reignest over all; and in thine hand is power and might; and in thine hand it is to make great, and to give strength unto all.* — 1 CHRONICLES 29:12

When I am tempted to put my trust in money, God's Word reminds me that. . .

....

....

....

....

....

....

....

....

....

....

....

....

....

....

253. *O that there were such an heart in them, that they would fear me, and keep all my commandments always, that it might be well with them, and with their children for ever!* — DEUTERONOMY 5:29

254. *If a man love me, he will keep my words: and my Father will love him, and we will come unto him, and make our abode with him.* — JOHN 14:23

255. *If ye keep my commandments, ye shall abide in my love; even as I have kept my Father's commandments, and abide in his love.* — JOHN 15:10

I *find* it most difficult to obey the Lord when. . .

....

....

....

....

....

....

....

....

....

....

....

....

....

....

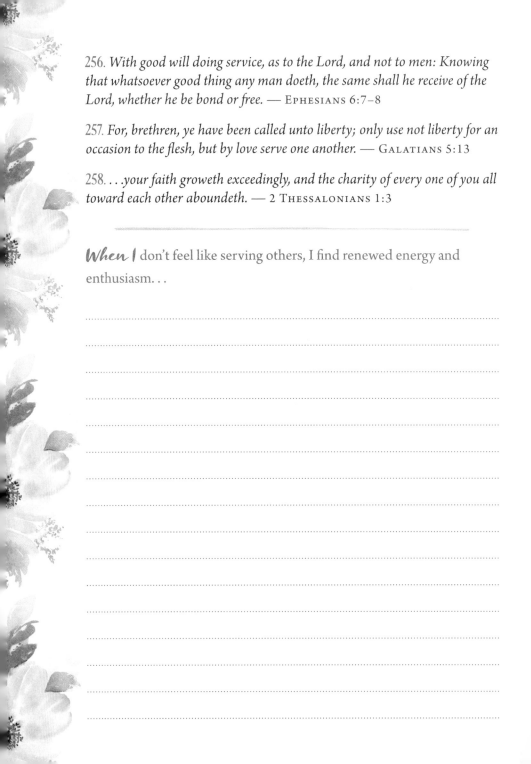

256. *With good will doing service, as to the Lord, and not to men: Knowing that whatsoever good thing any man doeth, the same shall he receive of the Lord, whether he be bond or free.* — Ephesians 6:7–8

257. *For, brethren, ye have been called unto liberty; only use not liberty for an occasion to the flesh, but by love serve one another.* — Galatians 5:13

258. *. . .your faith groweth exceedingly, and the charity of every one of you all toward each other aboundeth.* — 2 Thessalonians 1:3

When I don't feel like serving others, I find renewed energy and enthusiasm. . .

259. *Ask, and it shall be given you; seek, and ye shall find; knock, and it shall be opened unto you: for every one that asketh receiveth; and he that seeketh findeth.* — Matthew 7:7–8

260. *Whatsoever ye shall ask the Father in my name, he will give it you. Hitherto have ye asked nothing in my name: ask, and ye shall receive, that your joy may be full.* — John 16:23–24

261. *When thou hast shut thy door, pray to thy Father which is in secret; and thy Father which seeth in secret shall reward thee openly.* — Matthew 6:6

Talking to God about everything makes me feel. . .

....

....

....

....

....

....

....

....

....

....

....

....

....

....

....

262. *There hath no temptation taken you but such as is common to man: but God is faithful, who will not suffer you to be tempted above that ye are able; but will with the temptation also make a way to escape, that ye may be able to bear it.* — 1 CORINTHIANS 10:13

263. *Count it all joy when ye fall into divers temptations; knowing this, that the trying of your faith worketh patience.* — JAMES 1:2–3

264. *The Lord knoweth how to deliver the godly out of temptations, and to reserve the unjust unto the day of judgment to be punished.* — 2 PETER 2:9

I trust that the Lord will deliver me from temptation because. . .

....
....
....
....
....
....
....
....
....
....
....
....
....
....
....
....

265. *Let my heart be sound in thy statutes; that I be not ashamed.*
— PSALM 119:80

266. *As it is written, Behold, I lay in Sion a stumblingstone and rock of offence: and whosoever believeth on him shall not be ashamed.* — ROMANS 9:33

267. *And hope maketh not ashamed; because the love of God is shed abroad in our hearts by the Holy Ghost which is given unto us.* — ROMANS 5:5

I can forever be free from guilt and shame because. . .

268. *Is any sick among you? let him call for the elders of the church; and let them pray over him, anointing him with oil in the name of the Lord.*
— James 5:14

269. *But he was wounded for our transgressions, he was bruised for our iniquities: the chastisement of our peace was upon him; and with his stripes we are healed.* — Isaiah 53:5

270. *And ye shall serve the LORD your God, and he shall bless thy bread, and thy water; and I will take sickness away from the midst of thee.*
— Exodus 23:25

When I choose healthy eating and sleeping habits, I. . .

....
....
....
....
....
....
....
....
....
....
....
....
....
....

271. *Commit thy way unto the* Lord; *trust also in him; and he shall bring it to pass.* — Psalm 37:5

272. *They that trust in the* Lord *shall be as mount Zion, which cannot be removed, but abideth for ever.* — Psalm 125:1

273. *If any man trust to himself that he is Christ's, let him of himself think this again, that, as he is Christ's, even so are we Christ's.* — 2 Corinthians 10:7

My trust in the Lord grows when. . .

. . . .

. . . .

. . . .

. . . .

. . . .

. . . .

. . . .

. . . .

. . . .

. . . .

. . . .

. . . .

. . . .

. . . .

. . . .

274. *I will instruct thee and teach thee in the way which thou shalt go: I will guide thee with mine eye.* — PSALM 32:8

275. *I will bless the LORD, who hath given me counsel: my reins also instruct me in the night seasons.* — PSALM 16:7

276. *For God, who commanded the light to shine out of darkness, hath shined in our hearts, to give the light of the knowledge of the glory of God in the face of Jesus Christ.* — 2 CORINTHIANS 4:6

I remember a time the Lord provided me with His wisdom. . .

277. *Be ye strong therefore, and let not your hands be weak: for your work shall be rewarded.* — 2 CHRONICLES 15:7

278. *And God blessed the seventh day, and sanctified it: because that in it he had rested from all his work which God created and made.* — GENESIS 2:3

279. *Even a child is known by his doings, whether his work be pure, and whether it be right.* — PROVERBS 20:11

I can take pride in my work because. . .

280. *For in the time of trouble he shall hide me in his pavilion: in the secret of his tabernacle shall he hide me; he shall set me up upon a rock.*
— Psalm 27:5

281. *And we know that all things work together for good to them that love God, to them who are the called according to his purpose.* — Romans 8:28

282. *The righteous cry, and the Lord heareth, and delivereth them out of all their troubles.* — Psalm 34:17

I remember a time when God worked something difficult in my life out for good. . .

....
....
....
....
....
....
....
....
....
....
....
....
....
....
....
....

283. This book of the law shall not depart out of thy mouth; but thou shalt meditate therein day and night, that thou mayest observe to do according to all that is written therein. — JOSHUA 1:8

284. Therefore shall ye lay up these my words in your heart and in your soul, and bind them for a sign upon your hand, that they may be as frontlets between your eyes. — DEUTERONOMY 11:18

285. As newborn babes, desire the sincere milk of the word, that ye may grow thereby. — 1 PETER 2:2

My favorite way to study the Bible is. . .

....
....
....
....
....
....
....
....
....
....
....
....
....
....
....
....

286. *By humility and the fear of the Lord are riches, and honour, and life.* — PROVERBS 22:4

287. *Riches and honour are with me; yea, durable riches and righteousness. My fruit is better than gold, yea, than fine gold; and my revenue than choice silver.* — PROVERBS 8:18–19

288. *For thou shalt eat the labour of thine hands: happy shalt thou be, and it shall be well with thee.* — PSALM 128:2

I feel most successful when. . .

....

....

....

....

....

....

....

....

....

....

....

....

....

....

....

....

....

289. *This is a faithful saying, and worthy of all acceptation, that Christ Jesus came into the world to save sinners; of whom I am chief.* — 1 Timothy 1:15

290. *Who is a God like unto thee, that pardoneth iniquity, and passeth by the transgression of the remnant of his heritage? he retaineth not his anger for ever, because he delighteth in mercy.* — Micah 7:18

291. *But God, who is rich in mercy, for his great love wherewith he loved us...* — Ephesians 2:4

God continually shows His love and acceptance of me by. . .

....

....

....

....

....

....

....

....

....

....

....

....

....

....

....

292. *And she shall bring forth a son, and thou shalt call his name Jesus: for he shall save his people from their sins.* — MATTHEW 1:21

293. *Who gave himself for our sins, that he might deliver us from this present evil world, according to the will of God and our Father.* — GALATIANS 1:4

294. *In whom we have redemption through his blood, the forgiveness of sins, according to the riches of his grace.* — EPHESIANS 1:7

When I think about how Jesus redeemed me by His own blood. . .

....

....

....

....

....

....

....

....

....

....

....

....

....

....

....

....

....

295. *We have an advocate with the Father, Jesus Christ the righteous: and he is the propitiation for our sins: and not for ours only, but also for the sins of the whole world.* — 1 JOHN 2:1–2

296. *Who his own self bare our sins in his own body on the tree, that we, being dead to sins, should live unto righteousness: by whose stripes ye were healed.* — 1 PETER 2:24

297. *The next day John seeth Jesus coming unto him, and saith, Behold the Lamb of God, which taketh away the sin of the world.* — JOHN 1:29

My freedom in Christ exists because. . .

....

....

....

....

....

....

....

....

....

....

....

....

....

....

298. *Woe unto them that are wise in their own eyes, and prudent in their own sight!* — Isaiah 5:21

299. *Seest thou a man wise in his own conceit? there is more hope of a fool than of him.* — Proverbs 26:12

300. *He that trusteth in his own heart is a fool: but whoso walketh wisely, he shall be delivered.* — Proverbs 28:26

When I begin to think I am wise in my own eyes, God will. . .

....

....

....

....

....

....

....

....

....

....

....

....

....

....

301. *The* Lord *is with you, while ye be with him; and if ye seek him, he will be found of you; but if ye forsake him, he will forsake you.* — 2 Chronicles 15:2

302. *But if from thence thou shalt seek the* Lord *thy God, thou shalt find him, if thou seek him with all thy heart and with all thy soul.* — Deuteronomy 4:29

303. *Seek good, and not evil, that ye may live: and so the* Lord, *the God of hosts, shall be with you, as ye have spoken.* — Amos 5:14

When I put God at the top of my priority list. . .

....

....

....

....

....

....

....

....

....

....

....

....

....

....

....

....

....

304. *For this is good and acceptable in the sight of God our Saviour; who will have all men to be saved, and to come unto the knowledge of the truth.*
— 1 Timothy 2:3–4

305. *For therefore we both labour and suffer reproach, because we trust in the living God, who is the Saviour of all men, specially of those that believe.*
— 1 Timothy 4:9–10

306. *And in very deed for this cause have I raised thee up, for to shew in thee my power; and that my name may be declared throughout all the earth.*
— Exodus 9:16

My salvation comes with great purpose. . .

307. The LORD shall preserve thee from all evil: he shall preserve thy soul. The LORD shall preserve thy going out and thy coming in from this time forth, and even for evermore. — PSALM 121:7–8

308. The beloved of the LORD shall dwell in safety by him; and the Lord shall cover him all the day long, and he shall dwell between his shoulders.
— DEUTERONOMY 33:12

309. Because thou hast made the LORD, which is my refuge, even the most High, thy habitation; there shall no evil befall thee, neither shall any plague come nigh thy dwelling. — PSALM 91:9–10

My prayer of thanks for God's love and protection is this. . .

....

....

....

....

....

....

....

....

....

....

....

....

....

310. *He brought them out of darkness and the shadow of death, and brake their bands in sunder.* — PSALM 107:14

311. *Even the captives of the mighty shall be taken away, and the prey of the terrible shall be delivered: for I will contend with him that contendeth with thee, and I will save thy children.* — ISAIAH 49:25

312. *Which executeth judgment for the oppressed: which giveth food to the hungry. The LORD looseth the prisoners.* — PSALM 146:7

Because of my personal relationship with Christ, I am no longer a prisoner to. . .

313. *And this is the confidence that we have in him, that, if we ask any thing according to his will, he heareth us.* — 1 JOHN 5:14

314. *And if we know that he hear us, whatsoever we ask, we know that we have the petitions that we desired of him.* — 1 JOHN 5:15

315. *The effectual fervent prayer of a righteous man availeth much.* — JAMES 5:16

Without the gift of prayer, my life would be. . .

....

....

....

....

....

....

....

....

....

....

....

....

....

....

....

....

....

....

316. *Sing unto the LORD, praise ye the LORD: for he hath delivered the soul of the poor from the hand of evildoers.* — JEREMIAH 20:13

317. *For the LORD heareth the poor, and despiseth not his prisoners.* — PSALM 69:33

318. *For he shall deliver the needy when he crieth; the poor also, and him that hath no helper. He shall spare the poor and needy, and shall save the souls of the needy.* — PSALM 72:12–13

When times are tough financially, I will continue to hope because. . .

....

....

....

....

....

....

....

....

....

....

....

....

....

....

319. *Rejoicing in hope; patient in tribulation; continuing instant in prayer.*
— ROMANS 12:12

320. *For what glory is it, if, when ye be buffeted for your faults, ye shall take it patiently? but if, when ye do well, and suffer for it, ye take it patiently, this is acceptable with God.* — 1 PETER 2:20

321. *Rest in the LORD, and wait patiently for him: fret not thyself because of him who prospereth in his way, because of the man who bringeth wicked devices to pass.* — PSALM 37:7

The Lord helps me to wait patiently. . .

....

....

....

....

....

....

....

....

....

....

....

....

....

....

322. *That I may cause those that love me to inherit substance; and I will fill their treasures.* — PROVERBS 8:21

323. *I love them that love me; and those that seek me early shall find me.* — PROVERBS 8:17

324. *Know therefore that the LORD thy God, he is God, the faithful God, which keepeth covenant and mercy with them that love him and keep his commandments to a thousand generations.* — DEUTERONOMY 7:9

My love for God is. . .

....

....

....

....

....

....

....

....

....

....

....

....

....

....

....

325. *And, behold, I am with thee, and will keep thee in all places whither thou goest, and will bring thee again into this land; for I will not leave thee.* — GENESIS 28:15

326. *But I am poor and needy; yet the Lord thinketh upon me: thou art my help and my deliverer; make no tarrying, O my God.* — PSALM 40:17

327. *Since thou wast precious in my sight, thou hast been honourable, and I have loved thee.* — ISAIAH 43:4

I know God is always with me because. . .

....

....

....

....

....

....

....

....

....

....

....

....

....

....

....

328. *He that tilleth his land shall have plenty of bread: but he that followeth after vain persons shall have poverty enough.* — Proverbs 28:19

329. *Love not sleep, lest thou come to poverty; open thine eyes, and thou shalt be satisfied with bread.* — Proverbs 20:13

330. *The soul of the sluggard desireth, and hath nothing: but the soul of the diligent shall be made fat.* — Proverbs 13:4

When I'm tempted to be lazy, God's Word reminds me. . .

....

....

....

....

....

....

....

....

....

....

....

....

....

....

331. *Blessed is the people that know the joyful sound: they shall walk, O Lord, in the light of thy countenance.* — Psalm 89:15

332. *In thy name shall they rejoice all the day: in thy righteousness shall they be exalted.* — Psalm 89:16

333. *They that sow in tears shall reap in joy. He that goeth forth and weepeth, bearing precious seed, shall doubtless come again with rejoicing, bringing his sheaves with him.* — Psalm 126:5–6

Things that remind me to delight in the Lord's presence include. . .

334. *Remember the words of the Lord Jesus, how he said, It is more blessed to give than to receive.* — ACTS 20:35

335. *But whoso hath this world's good, and seeth his brother have need, and shutteth up his bowels of compassion from him, how dwelleth the love of God in him?* — 1 JOHN 3:17

336. *Distributing to the necessity of saints; given to hospitality.* — ROMANS 12:13

When I welcome others with love and appreciation, I feel. . .

....

....

....

....

....

....

....

....

....

....

....

....

....

....

....

....

....

....

....

337. *And I will pray the Father, and he shall give you another Comforter, that he may abide with you for ever.* — JOHN 14:16

338. *If ye then, being evil, know how to give good gifts unto your children: how much more shall your heavenly Father give the Holy Spirit to them that ask him?* — LUKE 11:13

339. *And I will put my spirit within you, and cause you to walk in my statutes, and ye shall keep my judgments, and do them.* — EZEKIEL 36:27

When I think about the Holy Spirit, my comforter. . .

....

....

....

....

....

....

....

....

....

....

....

....

....

....

340. *Have not I commanded thee? Be strong and of a good courage; be not afraid, neither be thou dismayed: for the LORD thy God is with thee whithersoever thou goest.* — JOSHUA 1:9

341. *My flesh and my heart faileth: but God is the strength of my heart, and my portion for ever.* — PSALM 73:26

342. *The LORD is my strength and my shield; my heart trusted in him, and I am helped: therefore my heart greatly rejoiceth; and with my song will I praise him.* — PSALM 28:7

When I face challenges, I find encouragement and hope in. . .

343. *But we all, with open face beholding as in a glass the glory of the Lord, are changed into the same image from glory to glory, even as by the Spirit of the Lord.* — 2 CORINTHIANS 3:18

344. *But the path of the just is as the shining light, that shineth more and more unto the perfect day.* — PROVERBS 4:18

345. *And this I pray, that your love may abound yet more and more in knowledge and in all judgment.* — PHILIPPIANS 1:9

It's important to extend grace to others because. . .

346. *My words shall be of the uprightness of my heart: and my lips shall utter knowledge clearly.* — Job 33:3

347. *The words of a wise man's mouth are gracious; but the lips of a fool will swallow up himself.* — Ecclesiastes 10:12

348. *In the multitude of words there wanteth not sin: but he that refraineth his lips is wise.* — Proverbs 10:19

Words matter because...

....
....
....
....
....
....
....
....
....
....
....
....
....
....
....
....
....
....

349. *He that goeth about as a talebearer revealeth secrets: therefore meddle not with him that flattereth with his lips.* — PROVERBS 20:19

350. *A froward man soweth strife: and a whisperer separateth chief friends.* — PROVERBS 16:28

351. *Keep thy tongue from evil, and thy lips from speaking guile.* — PSALM 34:13

It's important to think before I speak because. . .

352. *Therefore if thine enemy hunger, feed him; if he thirst, give him drink.*
— ROMANS 12:20

353. *To the Lord our God belong mercies and forgivenesses, though we have rebelled against him.* — DANIEL 9:9

354. *But if ye forgive not men their trespasses, neither will your Father forgive your trespasses.* — MATTHEW 6:15

When I think about how God wants me to love my enemies, I feel. . .

355. *A new commandment I give unto you, That ye love one another; as I have loved you, that ye also love one another.* — JOHN 13:34

356. *By this shall all men know that ye are my disciples, if ye have love one to another.* — JOHN 13:35

357. *A friend loveth at all times, and a brother is born for adversity.*
— PROVERBS 17:17

When I think about my friendships. . .

....
....
....
....
....
....
....
....
....
....
....
....
....
....
....
....
....

358. The LORD thy God will make thee plenteous in every work of thine hand, in the fruit of thy body, and in the fruit of thy cattle, and in the fruit of thy land. — DEUTERONOMY 30:9

359. God hath given riches and wealth, and hath given him power to eat thereof, and to take his portion, and to rejoice in his labour; this is the gift of God. — ECCLESIASTES 5:19

360. He shall be like a tree planted by the rivers of water, that bringeth forth his fruit in his season; his leaf also shall not wither; and whatsoever he doeth shall prosper. — PSALM 1:3

My success is not my own; it belongs to God because. . .

....

....

....

....

....

....

....

....

....

....

....

....

....

....

361. *According as his divine power hath given unto us all things that pertain unto life and godliness, through the knowledge of him that hath called us to glory and virtue.* — 2 PETER 1:3

362. *Wealth and riches shall be in his house: and his righteousness endureth for ever.* — PSALM 112:3

363. *And I will send grass in thy fields for thy cattle, that thou mayest eat and be full.* — DEUTERONOMY 11:15

God has always provided for me. . .

....
....
....
....
....
....
....
....
....
....
....
....
....
....
....

364. *God is our refuge and strength, a very present help in trouble. Therefore will not we fear, though the earth be removed, and though the mountains be carried into the midst of the sea.* — PSALM 46:1–2

365. *Behold, God is mine helper: the Lord is with them that uphold my soul.* — PSALM 54:4

366. *The LORD preserveth the simple: I was brought low, and he helped me.* — PSALM 116:6

Sometimes trust doesn't come easily because. . .

367. *Behold, thou desirest truth in the inward parts: and in the hidden part thou shalt make me to know wisdom.* — PSALM 51:6

368. *Evil men understand not judgment: but they that seek the LORD understand all things.* — PROVERBS 28:5

369. *For the LORD giveth wisdom: out of his mouth cometh knowledge and understanding. He layeth up sound wisdom for righteous: he is a buckler to them that walk uprightly.* — PROVERBS 2:6–7

When I don't know what to do, God's Word shows me. . .

....

....

....

....

....

....

....

....

....

....

....

....

....

....

....

370. *The holy scriptures, which are able to make thee wise unto salvation through faith which is in Christ Jesus.* — 2 TIMOTHY 3:15

371. *All scripture is given by inspiration of God, and is profitable for doctrine, for reproof, for correction, for instruction in righteousness.* — 2 TIMOTHY 3:16

372. *Thy word is a lamp unto my feet, and a light unto my path.* — PSALM 119:105

It's so important to know and understand God's promises because. . .

....

....

....

....

....

....

....

....

....

....

....

....

....

....

....

373. *Heaven and earth shall pass away, but my words shall not pass away.* — MATTHEW 24:35

374. *And now, brethren, I commend you to God, and to the word of his grace, which is able to build you up, and to give you an inheritance among all them which are sanctified.* — ACTS 20:32

375. *He that is of God heareth God's words.* — JOHN 8:47

Because of God's Word, I. . .

....

....

....

....

....

....

....

....

....

....

....

....

....

....

....

....

....

....

376. *I acknowledge my sin unto thee, and mine iniquity have I not hid. I said, I will confess my transgressions unto the LORD; and thou forgavest the iniquity of my sin.* — PSALM 32:5

377. *And they went out, and preached that men should repent.* — MARK 6:12

378. *He healeth the broken in heart, and bindeth up their wounds.* — PSALM 147:3

When I tell God I'm sorry, I feel. . .

379. *If thou shalt confess with thy mouth the Lord Jesus, and shalt believe in thine heart that God hath raised him from the dead, thou shalt be saved.*
— ROMANS 10:9

380. *So that a man shall say, Verily there is a reward for the righteous.*
— PSALM 58:11

381. *For thou, LORD, wilt bless the righteous; with favour wilt thou compass him as with a shield.* — PSALM 5:12

My heart is made right with God when. . .

....

....

....

....

....

....

....

....

....

....

....

....

....

....

....

382. But without faith it is impossible to please him: for he that cometh to God must believe that he is, and that he is a rewarder of them that diligently seek him. — HEBREWS 11:6

383. The hand of our God is upon all them for good that seek him; but his power and his wrath is against all them that forsake him. — EZRA 8:22

384. For thus saith the LORD unto the house of Israel, Seek ye me, and ye shall live. — AMOS 5:4

My greatest treasure. . .

....

....

....

....

....

....

....

....

....

....

....

....

....

....

....

....

....

385. *For this is the will of God, even your sanctification, that ye should abstain from fornication.* — 1 Thessalonians 4:3

386. *Know ye not that your bodies are the members of Christ? shall I then take the members of Christ, and make them the members of an harlot? God forbid.* — 1 Corinthians 6:15

387. *Who can find a virtuous woman? for her price is far above rubies.* — Proverbs 31:10

Because my body belongs to God, I will. . .

388. *For sin shall not have dominion over you: for ye are not under the law, but under grace.* — ROMANS 6:14

389. *Likewise reckon ye also yourselves to be dead indeed unto sin, but alive unto God through Jesus Christ our Lord.* — ROMANS 6:11

390. *Knowing this, that our old man is crucified with him, that the body of sin might be destroyed, that henceforth we should not serve sin. For he that is dead is freed from sin.* — ROMANS 6:6–7

Knowing I am free from my past. . .

....

....

....

....

....

....

....

....

....

....

....

....

....

....

391. *In the multitude of my thoughts within me thy comforts delight my soul.* — PSALM 94:19

392. *But as for you, ye thought evil against me; but God meant it unto good, to bring to pass, as it is this day, to save much people alive.* — GENESIS 50:20

393. *Blessed be God, even the Father of our Lord Jesus Christ, the Father of all mercies, and the God of all comfort.* — 2 CORINTHIANS 1:3

I find comfort in. . .

....

....

....

....

....

....

....

....

....

....

....

....

....

....

....

....

394. *Being confident of this very thing, that he which hath begun a good work in you will perform it until the day of Jesus Christ.* — PHILIPPIANS 1:6

395. *And now, little children, abide in him; that, when he shall appear, we may have confidence, and not be ashamed before him at his coming.* — 1 JOHN 2:28

396. *Though an host should encamp against me, my heart shall not fear: though war should rise against me, in this will I be confident.* — PSALM 27:3

I struggle to find my confidence when. . .

....

....

....

....

....

....

....

....

....

....

....

....

....

....

....

397. *The fear of the Lord is the beginning of wisdom: a good understanding have all they that do his commandments: his praise endureth for ever.*
— Psalm 111:10

398. *Come and hear, all ye that fear God, and I will declare what he hath done for my soul.* — Psalm 66:16

399. *Submit yourselves to every ordinance of man for the Lord's sake.*
— 1 Peter 2:13

I will praise the Lord because. . .

....

....

....

....

....

....

....

....

....

....

....

....

....

....

....

....

....

400. *I have glorified thee on the earth: I have finished the work which thou gavest me to do. And now, O Father, glorify thou me with thine own self with the glory which I had with thee before the world was.* — JOHN 17:4–5

401. *Jesus saith unto them, My meat is to do the will of him that sent me, and to finish his work.* — JOHN 4:34

402. *Then said they unto him, What shall we do, that we might work the works of God? Jesus answered and said unto them, This is the work of God, that ye believe on him whom he hath sent.* — JOHN 6:28–29

When I give my best effort, I feel. . .

403. *And ye know that he was manifested to take away our sins; and in him is no sin.* — 1 JOHN 3:5

404. *For by one offering he hath perfected for ever them that are sanctified.* — HEBREWS 10:14

405. *Be it known unto you therefore, men and brethren, that through this man is preached unto you the forgiveness of sins.* — ACTS 13:38

When I think about Jesus taking the weight of all of my sins. . .

406. *Cease from anger, and forsake wrath: fret not thyself in any wise to do evil.* — PSALM 37:8

407. *A wrathful man stirreth up strife: but he that is slow to anger appeaseth strife.* — PROVERBS 15:18

408. *Wrath is cruel, and anger is outrageous; but who is able to stand before envy?* — PROVERBS 27:4

I can let go of all negativity in my life because. . .

....

....

....

....

....

....

....

....

....

....

....

....

....

....

....

....

409. *Verily, verily, I say unto you, He that believeth on me hath everlasting life.* — JOHN 6:47

410. *Wherefore also it is contained in the scripture, Behold, I lay in Zion a chief corner stone, elect, precious: and he that believeth on him shall not be confounded.* — 1 PETER 2:6

411. *And Jesus said unto them, I am the bread of life: he that cometh to me shall never hunger; and he that believeth on me shall never thirst.* — JOHN 6:35

I believe in Jesus because. . .

....

....

....

....

....

....

....

....

....

....

....

....

....

....

....

412. *Cast thy bread upon the waters: for thou shalt find it after many days.*
— ECCLESIASTES 11:1

413. *And if thou draw out thy soul to the hungry, and satisfy the afflicted soul; then shall thy light rise in obscurity, and thy darkness be as the noon day.* — ISAIAH 58:10

414. *One thing thou lackest: go thy way, sell whatsoever thou hast, and give to the poor, and thou shalt have treasure in heaven: and come, take up the cross, and follow me.* — MARK 10:21

I can stop selfishness in its tracks when I...

....

....

....

....

....

....

....

....

....

....

....

....

....

....

415. *A wise son heareth his father's instruction: but a scorner heareth not rebuke.* — PROVERBS 13:1

416. *Children, obey your parents in the Lord: for this is right. Honour thy father and mother; which is the first commandment with promise.* — EPHESIANS 6:1–2

417. *Let no man despise thy youth; but be thou an example of the believers, in word, in conversation, in charity, in spirit, in faith, in purity.* — 1 TIMOTHY 4:12

It's important for me to be a good Christian example in the world because. . .

....

....

....

....

....

....

....

....

....

....

....

....

....

....

418. *Thou shalt increase my greatness, and comfort me on every side.*
— Psalm 71:21

419. *For he hath not despised nor abhorred the affliction of the afflicted; neither hath he hid his face from him; but when he cried unto him, he heard.*
— Psalm 22:24

420. *Cast thy burden upon the Lord, and he shall sustain thee: he shall never suffer the righteous to be moved.* — Psalm 55:22

I remember a difficult time when God comforted me. . .

....
....
....
....
....
....
....
....
....
....
....
....
....
....
....
....

421. *Wait on the LORD: be of good courage, and he shall strengthen thine heart: wait, I say, on the LORD.* — PSALM 27:14

422. *For the LORD loveth judgment, and forsaketh not his saints; they are preserved for ever: but the seed of the wicked shall be cut off.* — PSALM 37:28

423. *But now thus saith the LORD that created thee, O Jacob, and he that formed thee, O Israel, Fear not: for I have redeemed thee, I have called thee by thy name: thou art mine.* — ISAIAH 43:1

I choose to live unafraid because. . .

....

....

....

....

....

....

....

....

....

....

....

....

....

....

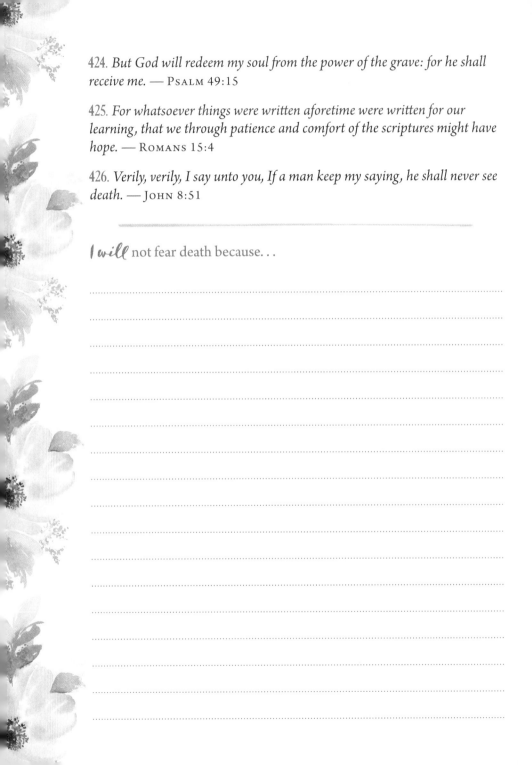

424. *But God will redeem my soul from the power of the grave: for he shall receive me.* — PSALM 49:15

425. *For whatsoever things were written aforetime were written for our learning, that we through patience and comfort of the scriptures might have hope.* — ROMANS 15:4

426. *Verily, verily, I say unto you, If a man keep my saying, he shall never see death.* — JOHN 8:51

I will not fear death because. . .

....
....
....
....
....
....
....
....
....
....
....
....
....
....
....
....
....
....

427. *And the* LORD *shall help them, and deliver them: he shall deliver them from the wicked, and save them, because they trust in him.* — PSALM 37:40

428. *For the rod of the wicked shall not rest upon the lot of the righteous; lest the righteous put forth their hands unto iniquity.* — PSALM 125:3

429. *The* LORD *hath sworn by his right hand, and by the arm of his strength, Surely I will no more give thy corn to be meat for thine enemies.* — ISAIAH 62:8

When it seems like my enemies are triumphant, God's Word reminds me that. . .

....

....

....

....

....

....

....

....

....

....

....

....

....

....

....

430. *And this is the promise that he hath promised us, even eternal life.*
— 1 John 2:25

431. *For since by man came death, by man came also the resurrection of the dead.* — 1 Corinthians 15:21

432. *And this is life eternal, that they might know thee the only true God, and Jesus Christ, whom thou hast sent.* — John 17:3

God's promise of eternal life means that. . .

....

....

....

....

....

....

....

....

....

....

....

....

....

....

433. *For we walk by faith, not by sight.* — 2 CORINTHIANS 5:7

434. *But let him ask in faith, nothing wavering. For he that wavereth is like a wave of the sea driven with the wind and tossed.* — JAMES 1:6

435. *And thou shalt be secure, because there is hope; yea, thou shalt dig about thee, and thou shalt take thy rest in safety.* — JOB 11:18

My faith means so much to me because. . .

....

....

....

....

....

....

....

....

....

....

....

....

....

....

....

436. *Let us draw near with a true heart in full assurance of faith, having our hearts sprinkled from an evil conscience, and our bodies washed with pure water.* — HEBREWS 10:22

437. *God is not a man, that he should lie; neither the son of man, that he should repent: hath he said, and shall he not do it?* — NUMBERS 23:19

438. *If we believe not, yet he abideth faithful: he cannot deny himself.* — 2 TIMOTHY 2:13

I've learned I can count on God because. . .

....

....

....

....

....

....

....

....

....

....

....

....

....

....

....

....

439. *Be not afraid of sudden fear, neither of the desolation of the wicked, when it cometh. For the LORD shall be thy confidence, and shall keep thy foot from being taken.* — PROVERBS 3:25–26

440. *Preaching the kingdom of God, and teaching those things which concern the Lord Jesus Christ, with all confidence...* — ACTS 28:31

441. *In righteousness shalt thou be established: thou shalt be far from oppression; for thou shalt not fear: and from terror; for it shall not come near thee.* — ISAIAH 54:14

I am confident in the Lord because He...

....

....

....

....

....

....

....

....

....

....

....

....

....

....

....

442. *A man's heart deviseth his way: but the LORD directeth his steps.*
— PROVERBS 16:9

443. *The righteousness of the perfect shall direct his way: but the wicked shall fall by his own wickedness.* — PROVERBS 11:5

444. *Thou shalt guide me with thy counsel, and afterward receive me to glory.*
— PSALM 73:24

When I recognize God is leading me I. . .

445. *Let the wicked forsake his way, and the unrighteous man his thoughts: and let him return unto the LORD, and he will have mercy upon him; and to our God, for he will abundantly pardon.* — ISAIAH 55:7

446. *For if our heart condemn us, God is greater than our heart, and knoweth all things.* — 1 JOHN 3:20

447. *For I will be merciful to their unrighteousness, and their sins and their iniquities will I remember no more.* — HEBREWS 8:12

When guilt tries to creep in, God reminds me that. . .

448. *Behold, his soul which is lifted up is not upright in him: but the just shall live by his faith.* — HABAKKUK 2:4

449. *If ye have faith, and doubt not. . .ye shall say unto this mountain, Be thou removed, and be thou cast into the sea; it shall be done.*
— MATTHEW 21:21

450. *He that believeth on him is not condemned: but he that believeth not is condemned already, because he hath not believed in the name of the only begotten Son of God.* — JOHN 3:18

I would define faith like this. . .

451. *Honour all men. Love the brotherhood. Fear God. Honour the king.*
— 1 Peter 2:17

452. *A gracious woman retaineth honour: and strong men retain riches.*
— Proverbs 11:16

453. *Honour thy father and thy mother.* — Luke 18:20

I want to show honor to others because. . .

....

....

....

....

....

....

....

....

....

....

....

....

....

....

....

....

....

....

454. *Though I walk in the midst of trouble, thou wilt revive me: thou shalt stretch forth thine hand against the wrath of mine enemies, and thy right hand shall save me.* — PSALM 138:7

455. *For as the sufferings of Christ abound in us, so our consolation also aboundeth by Christ.* — 2 CORINTHIANS 1:5

456. *The LORD is my rock, and my fortress, and my deliverer; my God, my strength, in whom I will trust; my buckler, and the horn of my salvation, and my high tower.* — PSALM 18:2

It is well with my soul because. . .

....

....

....

....

....

....

....

....

....

....

....

....

....

....

....

457. *Let your conversation be without covetousness; and be content with such things as ye have: for he hath said, I will never leave thee, nor forsake thee.* — HEBREWS 13:5

458. *Let not thine heart envy sinners: but be thou in the fear of the* LORD *all the day long. For surely there is an end; and thine expectation shall not be cut off.* — PROVERBS 23:17–18

459. *All the days of the afflicted are evil: but he that is of a merry heart hath a continual feast.* — PROVERBS 15:15

When I'm tempted to be envious of others. . .

....

....

....

....

....

....

....

....

....

....

....

....

....

....

....

....

460. As a man chasteneth his son, so the LORD thy God chasteneth thee. Therefore thou shalt keep the commandments of the LORD thy God, to walk in his ways, and to fear him. — DEUTERONOMY 8:5–6

461. Blessed is the man whom thou chastenest, O LORD, and teachest him out of thy law; that thou mayest give him rest from the days of adversity. — PSALM 94:12–13

462. For which cause we faint not; but though our outward man perish, yet the inward man is renewed day by day. — 2 CORINTHIANS 4:16

When my heart's not quite right, my prayer is this. . .

463. *Yea, though I walk through the valley of the shadow of death, I will fear no evil: for thou art with me; thy rod and thy staff they comfort me.*
— Psalm 23:4

464. *O death, where is thy sting? O grave, where is thy victory?*
— 1 Corinthians 15:55

465. *The wicked is driven away in his wickedness: but the righteous hath hope in his death.* — Proverbs 14:32

When I think about death, I find hope in. . .

466. *Thy right hand, O LORD, is become glorious in power: thy right hand, O LORD, hath dashed in pieces the enemy.* — EXODUS 15:6

467. *Through God we shall do valiantly: for he it is that shall tread down our enemies.* — PSALM 60:12

468. *That he would grant unto us, that we being delivered out of the hand of our enemies might serve him without fear.* — LUKE 1:74

When I think about God's awesome power, I feel. . .

469. *For the Lord himself shall descend from heaven with a shout, with the voice of the archangel, and with the trump of God: and the dead in Christ shall rise first.* — 1 THESSALONIANS 4:16

470. *For the hour is coming, in the which all that are in the graves shall hear his voice, and shall come forth; they that have done good, unto the resurrection of life.* — JOHN 5:28–29

471. *But if the Spirit of him that raised up Jesus from the dead dwell in you, he that raised up Christ from the dead shall also quicken your mortal bodies.* — ROMANS 8:11

I can share the good news of God's gift of eternal life with others by. . .

....

....

....

....

....

....

....

....

....

....

....

....

....

....

472. *Watch ye, stand fast in the faith, quit you like men, be strong.*
— 1 CORINTHIANS 16:13

473. *Be strong and of a good courage, fear not, nor be afraid of them: for the LORD thy God, he it is that doth go with thee; he will not fail thee, nor forsake thee.* — DEUTERONOMY 31:6

474. *It is God that girdeth me with strength, and maketh my way perfect.*
— PSALM 18:32

In moments when my faith wavers, I can find strength in. . .

....

....

....

....

....

....

....

....

....

....

....

....

....

....

475. The Lord is not slack concerning his promise, as some men count slackness; but is longsuffering to us-ward. — 2 Peter 3:9

476. And walk in love, as Christ also hath loved us, and hath given himself for us an offering and a sacrifice to God for a sweetsmelling savour. — Ephesians 5:2

477. Blessed be the Lord, that hath given rest unto his people Israel, according to all that he promised: there hath not failed one word of all his good promise. — 1 Kings 8:56

I know God's love never fails because. . .

478. *Fear not; for thou shalt not be ashamed: neither be thou confounded.*
— Isaiah 54:4

479. *I, even I, am he that comforteth you: who art thou, that thou shouldest be afraid of a man that shall die, and of the son of man which shall be made as grass.* — Isaiah 51:12

480. *There is no fear in love; but perfect love casteth out fear: because fear hath torment. He that feareth is not made perfect in love.* — 1 John 4:18

I can help others live fearlessly by. . .

....
....
....
....
....
....
....
....
....
....
....
....
....
....
....
....
....

481. *The righteous eateth to the satisfying of his soul: but the belly of the wicked shall want.* — PROVERBS 13:25

482. *He maketh peace in thy borders, and filleth thee with the finest of the wheat.* — PSALM 147:14

483. *Go to the ant, thou sluggard; consider her ways, and be wise: which having no guide, overseer, or ruler, provideth her meat in the summer, and gathereth her food in the harvest.* — PROVERBS 6:6–8

When I'm worried that I might not have what I need, this is my prayer. . .

....

....

....

....

....

....

....

....

....

....

....

....

....

....

....

484. *I am the vine, ye are the branches: he that abideth in me, and I in him, the same bringeth forth much fruit: for without me ye can do nothing.* — JOHN 15:5

485. *But now being made free from sin, and become servants to God, ye have your fruit unto holiness, and the end everlasting life.* — ROMANS 6:22

486. *They shall still bring forth fruit in old age; they shall be fat and flourishing.* — PSALM 92:14

I am most fruitful in my faith walk when. . .

487. *For I will forgive their iniquity, and I will remember their sin no more.* — JEREMIAH 31:34

488. *We know that we have passed from death unto life.* — 1 JOHN 3:14

489. *And I will cleanse them from all their iniquity, whereby they have sinned against me; and I will pardon all their iniquities, whereby they have sinned, and whereby they have transgressed against me.* — JEREMIAH 33:8

When I think about my past, I am thankful because. . .

....

....

....

....

....

....

....

....

....

....

....

....

....

....

....

....

490. *I will sing unto the LORD, because he hath dealt bountifully with me.* — PSALM 13:6

491. *There shall no evil befall thee, neither shall any plague come nigh thy dwelling. For he shall give his angels charge over thee, to keep thee in all thy ways.* — PSALM 91:10–11

492. *Why art thou cast down, O my soul? and why art thou disquieted within me? hope thou in God: for I shall yet praise him, who is the health of my countenance, and my God.* — PSALM 42:11

I will sing praises to God even in hard times because. . .

....
....
....
....
....
....
....
....
....
....
....
....
....
....
....
....

493. *Behold, I will pour out my spirit unto you, I will make known my words unto you.* — PROVERBS 1:23

494. *Even the Spirit of truth; whom the world cannot receive, because it seeth him not, neither knoweth him: but ye know him; for he dwelleth with you, and shall be in you.* — JOHN 14:17

495. *Howbeit when he, the Spirit of truth, is come, he will guide you into all truth. . .and he will shew you things to come.* — JOHN 16:13

I recognize the Holy Spirit is at work when. . .

....
....
....
....
....
....
....
....
....
....
....
....
....
....
....

496. *And the scripture was fulfilled which saith, Abraham believed God, and it was imputed unto him for righteousness: and he was called the Friend of God.* — James 2:23

497. *Be not deceived: evil communications corrupt good manners.* — 1 Corinthians 15:33

498. *Open rebuke is better than secret love. Faithful are the wounds of a friend; but the kisses of an enemy are deceitful.* — Proverbs 27:5–6

The qualities I want most in a friend include. . .

....

....

....

....

....

....

....

....

....

....

....

....

....

....

....

....

....

499. *And if thou sell ought unto thy neighbour, or buyest ought of thy neighbour's hand, ye shall not oppress one another.* — Leviticus 25:14

500. *Withhold not good from them to whom it is due, when it is in the power of thine hand to do it.* — Proverbs 3:27

501. *Ye shall not therefore oppress one another; but thou shalt fear thy God: for I am the Lord your God.* — Leviticus 25:17

I will treat others fairly because. . .

....

....

....

....

....

....

....

....

....

....

....

....

....

....

....

502. *Which is Christ in you, the hope of glory.* — Colossians 1:27

503. *For thou art my hope, O Lord God: thou art my trust from my youth.* — Psalm 71:5

504. *Wherefore gird up the loins of your mind, be sober, and hope to the end for the grace that is to be brought unto you at the revelation of Jesus Christ.* — 1 Peter 1:13

I can hold on to hope, no matter what, because. . .

....
....
....
....
....
....
....
....
....
....
....
....
....
....
....
....

505. *My soul shall be satisfied as with marrow and fatness; and my mouth shall praise thee with joyful lips.* — Psalm 63:5

506. *And thou shalt rejoice in the Lord, and shalt glory in the Holy One of Israel.* — Isaiah 41:16

507. *But let the righteous be glad; let them rejoice before God: yea, let them exceedingly rejoice.* — Psalm 68:3

My joy doesn't have to depend on how I feel but rather. . .

508. *I have been young, and now am old; yet have I not seen the righteous forsaken, nor his seed begging bread.* — PSALM 37:25

509. *Charge them that are rich in this world, that they be not highminded, nor trust in uncertain riches, but in the living God, who giveth us richly all things to enjoy.* — 1 TIMOTHY 6:17

510. *That they do good, that they be rich in good works, ready to distribute, willing to communicate.* — 1 TIMOTHY 6:18

My heart is sensitive to those in need, including. . .

....

....

....

....

....

....

....

....

....

....

....

....

....

511. *As arrows are in the hand of a mighty man; so are children of the youth. Happy is the man that hath his quiver full of them: they shall not be ashamed.* — Psalm 127:4–5

512. *Thy children like olive plants round about thy table.* — Psalm 128:3

513. *My son, if thine heart be wise, my heart shall rejoice, even mine. Yea, my reins shall rejoice, when thy lips speak right things.* — Proverbs 23:15–16

When I think about the children in my life. . .

514. The LORD hear thee in the day of trouble. — PSALM 20:1

515. The LORD also will be a refuge for the oppressed, a refuge in times of trouble. — PSALM 9:9

516. I will be glad and rejoice in thy mercy: for thou hast considered my trouble; thou hast known my soul in adversities. — PSALM 31:7

When my heart is heavy with burdens. . .

517. *And shall not God avenge his own elect, which cry day and night unto him, though he bear long with them?* — LUKE 18:7

518. *For the LORD your God is he that goeth with you, to fight for you against your enemies, to save you.* — DEUTERONOMY 20:4

519. *The LORD taketh my part with them that help me: therefore shall I see my desire upon them that hate me.* — PSALM 118:7

When life feels like a battle, I will remember this. . .

....

....

....

....

....

....

....

....

....

....

....

....

....

....

520. *Awake and sing, ye that dwell in dust: for thy dew is as the dew of herbs, and the earth shall cast out the dead.* — Isaiah 26:19

521. *And many of them that sleep in the dust of the earth shall awake, some to everlasting life, and some to shame and everlasting contempt.*
— Daniel 12:2

522. *In my flesh shall I see God: whom I shall see for myself, and mine eyes shall behold, and not another; though my reins be consumed within me.*
— Job 19:26–27

When I think about how my life is nothing more than a blink in time when compared to eternity. . .

....

....

....

....

....

....

....

....

....

....

....

....

....

....

523. *I will praise thy name; for thou hast done wonderful things; thy counsels of old are faithfulness and truth.* — ISAIAH 25:1

524. *Thy word is true from the beginning: and every one of thy righteous judgments endureth for ever.* — PSALM 119:160

525. *For ever, O LORD, thy word is settled in heaven. Thy faithfulness is unto all generations.* — PSALM 119:89–90

I know God never forgets His promises because. . .

....

....

....

....

....

....

....

....

....

....

....

....

....

....

526. *Herein is my Father glorified, that ye bear much fruit; so shall ye be my disciples.* — JOHN 15:8

527. *We beseech you, brethren, and exhort you by the Lord Jesus, that as ye have received of us how ye ought to walk and to please God, so ye would abound more and more.* — 1 THESSALONIANS 4:1

528. *The righteous also shall hold on his way, and he that hath clean hands shall be stronger and stronger.* — JOB 17:9

The fruits I see growing in my life include. . .

....

....

....

....

....

....

....

....

....

....

....

....

....

....

....

529. *I write unto you, little children, because your sins are forgiven you for his name's sake.* — 1 John 2:12

530. *But if we walk in the light, as he is in the light, we have fellowship one with another, and the blood of Jesus Christ his Son cleanseth us from all sin.* — 1 John 1:7

531. *I, even I, am he that blotteth out thy transgressions for mine own sake, and will not remember thy sins.* — Isaiah 43:25

With God, new beginnings are possible because. . .

....

....

....

....

....

....

....

....

....

....

....

....

....

....

532. *And call upon me in the day of trouble: I will deliver thee, and thou shalt glorify me.* — PSALM 50:15

533. *The LORD openeth the eyes of the blind: the LORD raiseth them that are bowed down: the LORD loveth the righteous.* — PSALM 146:8

534. *Thou, which hast shewed me great and sore troubles, shalt quicken me again, and shalt bring me up again from the depths of the earth.* — PSALM 71:20

I am thankful God holds my hand as I walk through the troubles in this life, because...

....

....

....

....

....

....

....

....

....

....

....

....

....

....

....

535. *That the blessing of Abraham might come on the Gentiles through Jesus Christ; that we might receive the promise of the Spirit through faith.*
— GALATIANS 3:14

536. *For the kingdom of God is not meat and drink; but righteousness, and peace, and joy in the Holy Ghost.* — ROMANS 14:17

537. *For ye have not received the spirit of bondage again to fear; but ye have received the Spirit of adoption, whereby we cry, Abba, Father.* — ROMANS 8:15

I recognize the Holy Spirit at work when. . .

....

....

....

....

....

....

....

....

....

....

....

....

....

....

....

538. *Lie not one to another, seeing that ye have put off the old man with his deeds; and have put on the new man, which is renewed in knowledge after the image of him that created him.* — Colossians 3:9–10

539. *The wicked borroweth, and payeth not again: but the righteous sheweth mercy, and giveth.* — Psalm 37:21

540. *He that walketh righteously, and speaketh uprightly; he that despiseth the gain of oppressions, that shaketh his hands from holding of bribes. . .he shall dwell on high.* — Isaiah 33:15–16

Because I want to keep my heart honest and pure, this is my prayer. . .

....

....

....

....

....

....

....

....

....

....

....

....

....

....

541. *Thou art my hiding place and my shield: I hope in thy word.* — Psalm 119:114

542. *A door was opened in heaven: and the first voice which I heard was as it were of a trumpet talking with me; which said, Come up hither, and I will shew thee things which must be hereafter.* — Revelation 4:1

543. *And every man that hath this hope in him purifieth himself, even as he is pure.* — 1 John 3:3

I have hope in the promise that this life is not all there is because. . .

....

....

....

....

....

....

....

....

....

....

....

....

....

....

....

....

544. *When he maketh inquisition for blood, he remembereth them: he forgetteth not the cry of the humble.* — Psalm 9:12

545. *Surely he scorneth the scorners: but he giveth grace unto the lowly.* — Proverbs 3:34

546. *Likewise, ye younger, submit yourselves unto the elder. Yea, all of you be subject one to another, and be clothed with humility: for God resisteth the proud, and giveth grace to the humble.* — 1 Peter 5:5

As I determine in my heart to point others to God, I will. . .

....
....
....
....
....
....
....
....
....
....
....
....
....
....
....

547. *For ye shall go out with joy. . .the mountains and the hills shall break forth before you into singing, and all the trees of the field shall clap their hands.* — Isaiah 55:12

548. *But the meek shall inherit the earth; and shall delight themselves in the abundance of peace.* — Psalm 37:11

549. *Light is sown for the righteous, and gladness for the upright in heart. Rejoice in the Lord, ye righteous; and give thanks at the remembrance of his holiness.* — Psalm 97:11–12

I take great pleasure in my relationship with the Lord because. . .

. . . .

. . . .

. . . .

. . . .

. . . .

. . . .

. . . .

. . . .

. . . .

. . . .

. . . .

. . . .

. . . .

. . . .

550. *And that ye study. . .to work with your own hands, as we commanded you; that ye may walk honestly toward them that are without, and that ye may have lack of nothing.* — 1 Thessalonians 4:11–12

551. *Not slothful in business; fervent in spirit; serving the Lord.* — Romans 12:11

552. *He that gathereth in summer is a wise son: but he that sleepeth in harvest is a son that causeth shame.* — Proverbs 10:5

I am blessed when I give my best for God because. . .

553. *The glory of young men is their strength: and the beauty of old men is the grey head.* — PROVERBS 20:29

554. *And thine age shall be clearer than the noonday: thou shalt shine forth, thou shalt be as the morning.* — JOB 11:17

555. *O God, forsake me not; until I have shewed thy strength unto this generation, and thy power to every one that is to come.* — PSALM 71:18

The promise of long life makes me feel. . .

556. *Be kindly affectioned one to another with brotherly love; in honour preferring one another.* — ROMANS 12:10

557. *Beloved, if God so loved us, we ought also to love one another.* — 1 JOHN 4:11

558. *My little children, let us not love in word, neither in tongue; but in deed and in truth.* — 1 JOHN 3:18

When I choose to love above all else. . .

....
....
....
....
....
....
....
....
....
....
....
....
....
....
....
....
....

559. The works of his hands are verity and judgment; all his commandments are sure. — PSALM 111:7

560. The LORD thy God in the midst of thee is mighty; he will save, he will rejoice over thee with joy; he will rest in his love, he will joy over thee with singing. — ZEPHANIAH 3:17

561. Yea, I will rejoice over them to do them good, and I will plant them in this land assuredly with my whole heart and with my whole soul. — JEREMIAH 32:41

Without God's love. . .

562. *For all that is in the world, the lust of the flesh, and the lust of the eyes, and the pride of life, is not of the Father, but is of the world.* — 1 JOHN 2:16

563. *And the world passeth away, and the lust thereof: but he that doeth the will of God abideth for ever.* — 1 JOHN 2:17

564. *Not by works of righteousness which we have done, but according to his mercy he saved us, by the washing of regeneration, and renewing of the Holy Ghost.* — TITUS 3:5

As I choose to submit my fleshly desires to the Lord. . .

565. *And ye shall not swear by my name falsely, neither shalt thou profane the name of thy God: I am the LORD.* — LEVITICUS 19:12

566. *Only fear the LORD, and serve him in truth with all your heart: for consider how great things he hath done for you.* — 1 SAMUEL 12:24

567. *A false witness shall not be unpunished, and he that speaketh lies shall perish.* — PROVERBS 19:9

I *find* that when I speak the truth, even though it's difficult. . .

....

....

....

....

....

....

....

....

....

....

....

....

....

....

568. *Husbands, love your wives, even as Christ also loved the church, and gave himself for it.* — Ephesians 5:25

569. *Drink waters out of thine own cistern, and running waters out of thine own well.* — Proverbs 5:15

570. *Let thy fountain be blessed: and rejoice with the wife of thy youth. Let her be as the loving hind and pleasant roe; let her breasts satisfy thee at all times.* — Proverbs 5:18–19

Marriage is important to God because. . .

....
....
....
....
....
....
....
....
....
....
....
....
....
....
....
....
....
....

571. *The meek shall eat and be satisfied: they shall praise the LORD that seek him: your heart shall live for ever.* — PSALM 22:26

572. *For the LORD taketh pleasure in his people: he will beautify the meek with salvation.* — PSALM 149:4

573. *Seek ye the LORD, all ye meek of the earth, which have wrought his judgment; seek righteousness, seek meekness: it may be ye shall be hid in the day of the LORD's anger.* — ZEPHANIAH 2:3

When I respond to others with kindness. . .

....

....

....

....

....

....

....

....

....

....

....

....

....

....

....

....

....

....

574. *And the LORD passed by before him, and proclaimed, The LORD, The LORD God, merciful and gracious, longsuffering, and abundant in goodness and truth, keeping mercy for thousands.* — EXODUS 34:6–7

575. *Like as a father pitieth his children, so the LORD pitieth them that fear him.* — PSALM 103:13

576. *Behold, the eye of the LORD is upon them that fear him, upon them that hope in his mercy.* — PSALM 33:18

This is what mercy means to me. . .

....

....

....

....

....

....

....

....

....

....

....

....

....

....

577. *Sell that ye have, and give alms; provide yourselves bags which wax not old, a treasure in the heavens that faileth not, where no thief approacheth, neither moth corrupteth.* — LUKE 12:33

578. *Every man according as he purposeth in his heart, so let him give; not grudgingly, or of necessity: for God loveth a cheerful giver.* — 2 CORINTHIANS 9:7

579. *Blessed is he that considereth the poor: the LORD will deliver him in time of trouble.* — PSALM 41:1

When I give to others with a cheerful heart. . .

....

....

....

....

....

....

....

....

....

....

....

....

....

....

....

....

....

....

....

....

580. *To do justice and judgment is more acceptable to the LORD than sacrifice.* — PROVERBS 21:3

581. *Thus saith the Lord GOD; Let it suffice you, O princes of Israel: remove violence and spoil, and execute judgment and justice, take away your exactions from my people, saith the Lord GOD.* — EZEKIEL 45:9

582. *The LORD bless thee, O habitation of justice, and mountain of holiness.* — JEREMIAH 31:23

I know I serve a just God because. . .

583. *Labour not to be rich: cease from thine own wisdom. Wilt thou set thine eyes upon that which is not? for riches certainly make themselves wings; they fly away as an eagle toward heaven.* — PROVERBS 23:4–5

584. *A little that a righteous man hath is better than the riches of many wicked.* — PSALM 37:16

585. *Hearken, my beloved brethren, hath not God chosen the poor of this world rich in faith, and heirs of the kingdom which he hath promised to them that love him?* — JAMES 2:5

My thoughts and feelings about money. . .

....

....

....

....

....

....

....

....

....

....

....

....

....

....

586. *I have set before thee this day life and good, and death and evil; in that I command thee this day to love the L*ORD *thy God, to walk in his ways, and to keep his commandments.* — DEUTERONOMY 30:15–16

587. *Therefore whosoever heareth these sayings of mine, and doeth them, I will liken him unto a wise man.* — MATTHEW 7:24

588. *And thou shalt do that which is right and good in the sight of the L*ORD*: that it may be well with thee, and that thou mayest go in and possess the good land which the L*ORD *sware unto thy fathers.* — DEUTERONOMY 6:18

Obedience is the very best way to live because. . .

....
....
....
....
....
....
....
....
....
....
....
....
....
....
....
....

589. *Be patient therefore, brethren, unto the coming of the Lord. Behold, the husbandman waiteth for the precious fruit of the earth, and hath long patience for it, until he receive the early and latter rain.* — JAMES 5:7

590. *But he that shall endure unto the end, the same shall be saved.* — MATTHEW 24:13

591. *But let patience have her perfect work, that ye may be perfect and entire, wanting nothing.* — JAMES 1:4

My prayer for patience is this. . .

....

....

....

....

....

....

....

....

....

....

....

....

....

....

592. *Peace, peace to him that is far off, and to him that is near, saith the* LORD; *and I will heal him.* — ISAIAH 57:19

593. *I will hear what God the* LORD *will speak: for he will speak peace unto his people, and to his saints.* — PSALM 85:8

594. *And let the peace of God rule in your hearts, to the which also ye are called in one body; and be ye thankful.* — COLOSSIANS 3:15

True peace is possible because...

....

....

....

....

....

....

....

....

....

....

....

....

....

....

....

....

595. *He will regard the prayer of the destitute, and not despise their prayer.* — PSALM 102:17

596. *He raiseth up the poor out of the dust, and lifteth the needy out of the dunghill.* — PSALM 113:7

597. *As sorrowful, yet alway rejoicing; as poor, yet making many rich; as having nothing, and yet possessing all things.* — 2 CORINTHIANS 6:10

"Poor" can refer to so much more than a lack of money, such as. . .

598. *Yet the* LORD *will command his lovingkindness in the day time, and in the night his song shall be with me, and my prayer unto the God of my life.*
— PSALM 42:8

599. *If ye abide in me, and my words abide in you, ye shall ask what ye will, and it shall be done unto you.* — JOHN 15:7

600. *And whatsoever ye shall ask in my name, that will I do, that the Father may be glorified in the Son. If ye shall ask any thing in my name, I will do it.*
— JOHN 14:13–14

A time I have witnessed the power of prayer. . .

....

....

....

....

....

....

....

....

....

....

....

....

....

....

601. *Whom having not seen, ye love; in whom, though now ye see him not, yet believing, ye rejoice with joy unspeakable and full of glory.* — 1 Peter 1:8

602. *Thou wilt shew me the path of life: in thy presence is fulness of joy; at thy right hand there are pleasures for evermore.* — Psalm 16:11

603. *Thou hast put gladness in my heart, more than in the time that their corn and their wine increased.* — Psalm 4:7

The joy of the Lord is my strength when. . .

....

....

....

....

....

....

....

....

....

....

....

....

....

....

....

604. *Look on every one that is proud, and bring him low; and tread down the wicked in their place.* — Job 40:12

605. *And God saw every thing that he had made, and, behold, it was very good.* — Genesis 1:31

606. *Therefore it shall come to pass, that as all good things are come upon you, which the Lord your God promised you.* — Joshua 23:15

It's important to remember *every good thing* comes from God because. . .

....
....
....
....
....
....
....
....
....
....
....
....
....
....
....
....
....
....
....

607. *When ye received the word of God which ye heard of us, ye received it not as the word of men, but as it is in truth, the word of God, which effectually worketh also in you that believe.* — 1 Thessalonians 2:13

608. *If any man speak, let him speak as the oracles of God; if any man minister, let him do it as of the ability which God giveth: that God in all things may be glorified through Jesus Christ.* — 1 Peter 4:11

609. *A man's belly shall be satisfied with the fruit of his mouth; and with the increase of his lips shall he be filled.* — Proverbs 18:20

When others speak God's truth into my life. . .

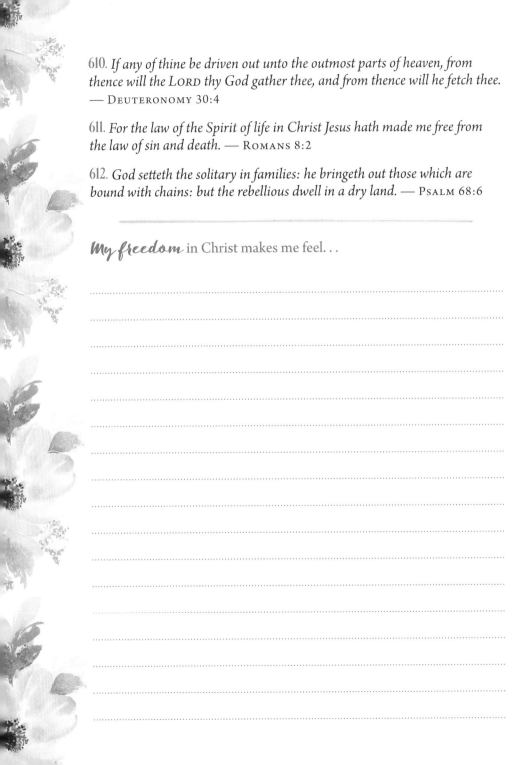

610. *If any of thine be driven out unto the outmost parts of heaven, from thence will the* LORD *thy God gather thee, and from thence will he fetch thee.* — DEUTERONOMY 30:4

611. *For the law of the Spirit of life in Christ Jesus hath made me free from the law of sin and death.* — ROMANS 8:2

612. *God setteth the solitary in families: he bringeth out those which are bound with chains: but the rebellious dwell in a dry land.* — PSALM 68:6

My freedom in Christ makes me feel. . .

613. *He shall not be afraid of evil tidings: his heart is fixed, trusting in the* LORD. — PSALM 112:7

614. *He maketh the storm a calm, so that the waves thereof are still.* — PSALM 107:29

615. *The* LORD *is my light and my salvation; whom shall I fear? the* LORD *is the strength of my life; of whom shall I be afraid?* — PSALM 27:1

When my heart shudders at the sound of bad news, I will. . .

....
....
....
....
....
....
....
....
....
....
....
....
....
....
....
....
....

616. *The fear of the wicked, it shall come upon him: but the desire of the righteous shall be granted.* — PROVERBS 10:24

617. *A good man obtaineth favour of the LORD: but a man of wicked devices will he condemn.* — PROVERBS 12:2

618. *Evil pursueth sinners: but to the righteous good shall be repayed.* — PROVERBS 13:21

Knowing that God has given me the right to stand before Him without fear of condemnation, I feel. . .

....

....

....

....

....

....

....

....

....

....

....

....

....

....

619. *An angry man stirreth up strife, and a furious man aboundeth in transgression.* — PROVERBS 29:22

620. *He that is soon angry dealeth foolishly.* — PROVERBS 14:17

621. *He that is slow to anger is better than the mighty; and he that ruleth his spirit than he that taketh a city.* — PROVERBS 16:32

When I feel anger rising within my spirit, God's Word reminds me. . .

622. *I am crucified with Christ: nevertheless I live; yet not I, but Christ liveth in me: and the life which I now live in the flesh.* — GALATIANS 2:20

623. *I live by the faith of the Son of God, who loved me, and gave himself for me.* — GALATIANS 2:20

624. *And Jesus answering saith unto them, Have faith in God.* — MARK 11:22

One of the best ways to deepen my faith is. . .

625. *Say ye to the righteous, that it shall be well with him: for they shall eat the fruit of their doings.* — Isaiah 3:10

626. *Surely goodness and mercy shall follow me all the days of my life: and I will dwell in the house of the Lord for ever.* — Psalm 23:6

627. *Salvation belongeth unto the Lord: thy blessing is upon thy people.* — Psalm 3:8

When I think of the favor God has lavishly poured upon me. . .

....

....

....

....

....

....

....

....

....

....

....

....

....

....

....

....

....

....

628. *There is a generation that are pure in their own eyes, and yet is not washed from their filthiness. There is a generation, O how lofty are their eyes! and their eyelids are lifted up.* — Proverbs 30:12–13

629. *Yet thou sayest, Because I am innocent, surely his anger shall turn from me. Behold, I will plead with thee, because thou sayest, I have not sinned.* — Jeremiah 2:35

630. *But he that glorieth, let him glory in the Lord. For not he that commendeth himself is approved, but whom the Lord commendeth.* — 2 Corinthians 10:17–18

When I am tempted to see myself as "righteous" in my own eyes, God's Word calls me to. . .

631. *He that is of a proud heart stirreth up strife: but he that putteth his trust in the LORD shall be made fat.* — PROVERBS 28:25

632. *Humble yourselves in the sight of the Lord, and he shall lift you up.* — JAMES 4:10

633. *But we are all as an unclean thing, and all our righteousnesses are as filthy rags; and we all do fade as a leaf; and our iniquities, like the wind, have taken us away.* — ISAIAH 64:6

The Lord helps to keep me humble by. . .

634. *I am not ashamed: for I know whom I have believed, and am persuaded that he is able to keep that which I have committed unto him against that day.* — 2 Timothy 1:12

635. *Study to shew thyself approved unto God, a workman that needeth not to be ashamed, rightly dividing the word of truth.* — 2 Timothy 2:15

636. *Looking unto Jesus. . .who for the joy that was set before him endured the cross, despising the shame, and is set down at the right hand of the throne of God.* — Hebrews 12:2

My heavenly Father has removed my shame, and my prayer of thanks to Him is this. . .

....

....

....

....

....

....

....

....

....

....

....

....

....

....

637. *I am the Lord that healeth thee.* — Exodus 15:26

638. *(Then saith [Jesus] to the sick of the palsy,) Arise, take up thy bed, and go unto thine house. And he arose, and departed to his house.* — Matthew 9:6–7

639. *Confess your faults one to another, and pray one for another, that ye may be healed.* — James 5:16

When I need healing, God will. . .

....

....

....

....

....

....

....

....

....

....

....

....

....

....

640. *If ye be reproached for the name of Christ, happy are ye; for the spirit of glory and of God resteth upon you: on their part he is evil spoken of, but on your part he is glorified.* — 1 PETER 4:14

641. *Blessed are ye, when men shall revile you, and persecute you, and shall say all manner of evil against you falsely, for my sake.* — MATTHEW 5:11

642. *Rejoice, and be exceeding glad: for great is your reward in heaven: for so persecuted they the prophets which were before you.* — MATTHEW 5:12

When I feel persecuted, scripture reminds me that. . .

....

....

....

....

....

....

....

....

....

....

....

....

....

....

....

643. *We have also a more sure word of prophecy; whereunto ye do well that ye take heed, as unto a light that shineth in a dark place, until the day dawn, and the day star arise in your hearts.* — 2 PETER 1:19

644. *Finally, brethren, pray for us, that the word of the Lord may have free course, and be glorified, even as it is with you.* — 2 THESSALONIANS 3:1

645. *For the word of God is quick, and powerful, and sharper than any twoedged sword. . .and is a discerner of the thoughts and intents of the heart.* — HEBREWS 4:12

God's Word illuminates my heart and guides me to. . .

....

....

....

....

....

....

....

....

....

....

....

....

....

....

646. *Now the God of peace. . .make you perfect in every good work to do his will, working in you that which is wellpleasing in his sight, through Jesus Christ; to whom be glory for ever and ever. Amen.* — HEBREWS 13:20–21

647. *For he shall be as a tree planted by the waters, and that spreadeth out her roots by the river, and shall not see when heat cometh, but her leaf shall be green.* — JEREMIAH 17:8

648. *Great peace have they which love thy law: and nothing shall offend them.* — PSALM 119:165

Knowing that my anxiety does not come from God, I will. . .

....
....
....
....
....
....
....
....
....
....
....
....
....
....
....

649. *O come, let us worship and bow down: let us kneel before the* LORD *our maker. For he is our God; and we are the people of his pasture, and the sheep of his hand.* — PSALM 95:6–7

650. *All nations whom thou hast made shall come and worship before thee, O Lord; and shall glorify thy name.* — PSALM 86:9

651. *Who shall not fear thee, O Lord, and glorify thy name? for thou only art holy: for all nations shall come and worship before thee; for thy judgments are made manifest.* — REVELATION 15:4

Taking time to praise God makes a difference in my life in many ways, including...

....

....

....

....

....

....

....

....

....

....

....

....

....

....

652. *The hope set before us: which hope we have as an anchor of the soul.*
— HEBREWS 6:18–19

653. *For in thee, O LORD, do I hope: thou wilt hear, O Lord my God.*
— PSALM 38:15

654. *Hope deferred maketh the heart sick: but when the desire cometh, it is a tree of life.* — PROVERBS 13:12

When hope anchors my soul. . .

....

....

....

....

....

....

....

....

....

....

....

....

....

....

....

....

....

655. *But when he saw the multitudes, he was moved with compassion on them, because they fainted, and were scattered abroad, as sheep having no shepherd.* — MATTHEW 9:36

656. *And Jesus went forth, and saw a great multitude, and was moved with compassion toward them, and he healed their sick.* — MATTHEW 14:14

657. *Shouldest not thou also have had compassion on thy fellowservant, even as I had pity on thee?* — MATTHEW 18:33

When my heart is filled with compassion for others, I. . .

658. *What doth it profit, my brethren, though a man say he hath faith, and have not works? can faith save him?* — JAMES 2:14

659. *Behold, I stand at the door, and knock: if any man hear my voice, and open the door, I will come in to him, and will sup with him, and he with me.* — REVELATION 3:20

660. *They profess that they know God; but in works they deny him, being abominable, and disobedient, and unto every good work reprobate.* — TITUS 1:16

When I give time to Jesus. . .

661. *Not forsaking the assembling of ourselves together, as the manner of some is; but exhorting one another: and so much the more, as ye see the day approaching.* — HEBREWS 10:25

662. *And when the day of Pentecost was fully come, they were all with one accord in one place.* — ACTS 2:1

663. *Wherefore comfort yourselves together, and edify one another, even as also ye do.* — 1 THESSALONIANS 5:11

When I gather with others who share my faith, I feel. . .

664. *I have fought a good fight, I have finished my course, I have kept the faith.* — 2 Timothy 4:7

665. *Keep thy heart with all diligence; for out of it are the issues of life.* — Proverbs 4:23

666. *And Jesus looking upon them saith, With men it is impossible, but not with God: for with God all things are possible.* — Mark 10:27

When I think about giving up, God nudges my heart to. . .

667. *But sanctify the Lord God in your hearts: and be ready always to give an answer to every man that asketh you a reason of the hope that is in you with meekness and fear.* — 1 Peter 3:15

668. *These are the things that ye shall do; speak ye every man the truth to his neighbour; execute the judgment of truth and peace in your gates.*
— Zechariah 8:16

669. *But speaking the truth in love, may grow up into him in all things, which is the head, even Christ.* — Ephesians 4:15

It's always important to speak the truth in love because. . .

....

....

....

....

....

....

....

....

....

....

....

....

....

....

....

....

670. *Trust in him at all times; ye people, pour out your heart before him: God is a refuge for us.* — Psalm 62:8

671. *He that dwelleth in the secret place of the most High shall abide under the shadow of the Almighty.* — Psalm 91:1

672. *Put on the whole armour of God, that ye may be able to stand against the wiles of the devil.* — Ephesians 6:11

When I need to feel safe, I pray. . .

673. *Death and life are in the power of the tongue: and they that love it shall eat the fruit thereof.* — PROVERBS 18:21

674. *Let no corrupt communication proceed out of your mouth, but that which is good to the use of edifying, that it may minister grace unto the hearers.* — EPHESIANS 4:29

675. *Neither filthiness, nor foolish talking, nor jesting, which are not convenient: but rather giving of thanks.* — EPHESIANS 5:4

Knowing that my words can contain life or death, I will choose to. . .

676. *That ye may be blameless and harmless, the sons of God, without rebuke, in the midst of a crooked and perverse nation, among whom ye shine as lights in the world.* — PHILIPPIANS 2:15

677. *Be not thou therefore ashamed of the testimony of our Lord, nor of me his prisoner: but be thou partaker of the afflictions of the gospel according to the power of God.* — 2 TIMOTHY 1:8

678. *And that repentance and remission of sins should be preached in his name among all nations, beginning at Jerusalem.* — LUKE 24:47

Sharing my faith with others makes me feel. . .

....
....
....
....
....
....
....
....
....
....
....
....
....
....
....
....

679. *Learn to do well; seek judgment, relieve the oppressed, judge the fatherless, plead for the widow.* — Isaiah 1:17

680. *Defend the poor and fatherless: do justice to the afflicted and needy.* — Psalm 82:3

681. *For if they fall, the one will lift up his fellow: but woe to him that is alone when he falleth; for he hath not another to help him up.* — Ecclesiastes 4:10

When I have the opportunity to stand up for others, I will choose to. . .

682. *Take heed to yourselves: if thy brother trespass against thee, rebuke him; and if he repent, forgive him.* — LUKE 17:3

683. *Stand fast therefore in the liberty wherewith Christ hath made us free, and be not entangled again with the yoke of bondage.* — GALATIANS 5:1

684. *But I say unto you, that every idle word that men shall speak, they shall give account thereof in the day of judgment.* — MATTHEW 12:36

When it's important to stand up for myself, I will choose to. . .

....

....

....

....

....

....

....

....

....

....

....

....

....

....

....

....

685. *Where sin abounded, grace did much more abound.* — Romans 5:20

686. *Then came Peter to him, and said, Lord, how oft shall my brother sin against me, and I forgive him? till seven times?* — Matthew 18:21

687. *And if by grace, then is it no more of works: otherwise grace is no more grace. But if it be of works, then it is no more grace: otherwise work is no more work.* — Romans 11:6

When I think about the many second chances I've been given, it makes me feel. . .

688. *Is any among you afflicted? let him pray. Is any merry? let him sing psalms.* — JAMES 5:13

689. *Praise ye the LORD: for it is good to sing praises unto our God; for it is pleasant; and praise is comely.* — PSALM 147:1

690. *Make a joyful noise unto the LORD, all ye lands.* — PSALM 100:1

When I carry a song of praise in my heart and on my lips, I feel. . .

691. *Therefore being justified by faith, we have peace with God through our Lord Jesus Christ.* — ROMANS 5:1

692. *And be not conformed to this world: but be ye transformed by the renewing of your mind, that ye may prove what is that good, and acceptable, and perfect, will of God.* — ROMANS 12:2

693. *And he withdrew himself into the wilderness, and prayed.* — LUKE 5:16

When I struggle with sleeplessness, I think about. . .

....

....

....

....

....

....

....

....

....

....

....

....

....

....

....

....

....

694. *I will praise thee; for I am fearfully and wonderfully made: marvellous are thy works; and that my soul knoweth right well.* — PSALM 139:14

695. *So God created man in his own image, in the image of God created he him; male and female created he them.* — GENESIS 1:27

696. *I beseech you therefore, brethren, by the mercies of God, that ye present your bodies a living sacrifice, holy, acceptable unto God, which is your reasonable service.* — ROMANS 12:1

When I struggle with my self-image, this is my prayer. . .

697. *The face of the LORD is against them that do evil, to cut off the remembrance of them from the earth.* — PSALM 34:16

698. *Ye that love the LORD, hate evil: he preserveth the souls of his saints; he delivereth them out of the hand of the wicked.* — PSALM 97:10

699. *The evil bow before the good; and the wicked at the gates of the righteous.* — PROVERBS 14:19

I know God will deliver me from evil because. . .

700. *Thou wilt keep him in perfect peace, whose mind is stayed on thee: because he trusteth in thee.* — ISAIAH 26:3

701. *Let the words of my mouth, and the meditation of my heart, be acceptable in thy sight, O LORD, my strength, and my redeemer.* — PSALM 19:14

702. *My meditation of him shall be sweet: I will be glad in the LORD.* — PSALM 104:34

When my thoughts and emotions spiral out of control. . .

....

....

....

....

....

....

....

....

....

....

....

....

....

....

703. *The law of his God is in his heart; none of his steps shall slide.*
— Psalm 37:31

704. *Thy word have I hid in mine heart, that I might not sin against thee.*
— Psalm 119:11

705. *But the scripture hath concluded all under sin, that the promise by faith of Jesus Christ might be given to them that believe.* — Galatians 3:22

Memorizing scripture impacts my life in many ways, including. . .

....

....

....

....

....

....

....

....

....

....

....

....

....

....

....

....

....

....

706. *By him therefore let us offer the sacrifice of praise to God continually, that is, the fruit of our lips giving thanks to his name. But to do good and to communicate forget not: for with such sacrifices God is well pleased.*
— HEBREWS 13:15–16

707. *Then Peter and the other apostles answered and said, We ought to obey God rather than men.* — ACTS 5:29

708. *Thus saith the LORD; Cursed be the man that trusteth in man, and maketh flesh his arm, and whose heart departeth from the LORD.*
— JEREMIAH 17:5

It's more important to please God than to please people because. . .

....
....
....
....
....
....
....
....
....
....
....
....
....
....

709. And God shall wipe away all tears from their eyes; and there shall be no more death, neither sorrow, nor crying, neither shall there be any more pain: for the former things are passed away. — REVELATION 21:4

710. For thou wilt not leave my soul in hell; neither wilt thou suffer thine Holy One to see corruption. — PSALM 16:10

711. In my Father's house are many mansions: if it were not so, I would have told you. I go to prepare a place for you. — JOHN 14:2

When I think about heaven, I imagine this is what it will be like...

....

....

....

....

....

....

....

....

....

....

....

....

....

....

....

....

712. The LORD hath appeared of old unto me, saying, Yea, I have loved thee with an everlasting love: therefore with lovingkindness have I drawn thee. — JEREMIAH 31:3

713. That Christ may dwell in your hearts by faith; that ye, being rooted and grounded in love. . . — EPHESIANS 3:17

714. Because he hath set his love upon me, therefore will I deliver him: I will set him on high, because he hath known my name. — PSALM 91:14

I love the Lord with all my heart because. . .

....

....

....

....

....

....

....

....

....

....

....

....

....

....

....

....

....

715. *And whosoever shall exalt himself shall be abased; and he that shall humble himself shall be exalted.* — MATTHEW 23:12

716. *LORD, thou hast heard the desire of the humble: thou wilt prepare their heart, thou wilt cause thine ear to hear.* — PSALM 10:17

717. *When men are cast down, then thou shalt say, There is lifting up; and he shall save the humble person.* — JOB 22:29

I honor the Lord when I am humble because. . .

718. *The fear of man bringeth a snare: but whoso putteth his trust in the* LORD *shall be safe.* — PROVERBS 29:25

719. *Fear thou not; for I am with thee: be not dismayed; for I am thy God: I will strengthen thee; yea, I will help thee; yea, I will uphold thee with the right hand of my righteousness.* — ISAIAH 41:10

720. *And the* LORD, *he it is that doth go before thee; he will be with thee, he will not fail thee, neither forsake thee: fear not, neither be dismayed.* — DEUTERONOMY 31:8

My faith will always overcome my fears because. . .

....

....

....

....

....

....

....

....

....

....

....

....

....

....

....

....

721. *And hereby we know that we are of the truth, and shall assure our hearts before him.* — 1 John 3:19

722. *That I might make thee know the certainty of the words of truth. . .* — Proverbs 22:21

723. *. . .yet will he have compassion according to the multitude of his mercies. For he doth not afflict willingly nor grieve the children of men.* — Lamentations 3:32–33

When I encounter difficulties, I am assured by God's Word that. . .

....

....

....

....

....

....

....

....

....

....

....

....

....

....

....

....

....

724. *My voice shalt thou hear in the morning, O LORD; in the morning will I direct my prayer unto thee, and will look up.* — PSALM 5:3

725. *And in the morning, rising up a great while before day, he went out, and departed into a solitary place, and there prayed.* — MARK 1:35

726. *Awake up, my glory; awake, psaltery and harp: I myself will awake early.* — PSALM 57:8

My morning prayer is this. . .

727 *So teach us to number our days, that we may apply our hearts unto wisdom.* — PSALM 90:12

728. *Walk in wisdom toward them that are without, redeeming the time.* — COLOSSIANS 4:5

729. *But seek ye first the kingdom of God, and his righteousness; and all these things shall be added unto you.* — MATTHEW 6:33

The Lord guides me to manage my time. . .

730. *Thy testimonies also are my delight and my counselors.* — Psalm 119:24

731. *Iron sharpeneth iron; so a man sharpeneth the countenance of his friend.* — Proverbs 27:17

732. *One generation shall praise thy works to another, and shall declare thy mighty acts.* — Psalm 145:4

My many godly mentors have influenced my life. . .

....

....

....

....

....

....

....

....

....

....

....

....

....

....

....

....

....

733. *For I know the thoughts that I think toward you, saith the LORD, thoughts of peace, and not of evil, to give you an expected end.* — JEREMIAH 29:11

734. *Let them shout for joy, and be glad, that favour my righteous cause: yea, let them say continually, Let the LORD be magnified, which hath pleasure in the prosperity of his servant.* — PSALM 35:27

735. *Not as though I had already attained, either were already perfect: but I follow after, if that I may apprehend that for which also I am apprehended of Christ Jesus.* — PHILIPPIANS 3:12

When I feel stuck, this is my prayer. . .

....

....

....

....

....

....

....

....

....

....

....

....

....

....

....

....

736. *And whatsoever ye do, do it heartily, as to the Lord, and not unto men; knowing that of the Lord ye shall receive the reward of the inheritance: for ye serve the Lord Christ.* — COLOSSIANS 3:23–24

737. *The husbandman that laboureth must be first partaker of the fruits.* — 2 TIMOTHY 2:6

738. *Much food is in the tillage of the poor: but there is that is destroyed for want of judgment.* — PROVERBS 13:23

The Lord blesses hard workers because. . .

739. *Let all bitterness, and wrath, and anger, and clamour, and evil speaking, be put away from you, with all malice: and be ye kind one to another, tenderhearted, forgiving one another.* — EPHESIANS 4:31–32

740. *Follow peace with all men, and holiness, without which no man shall see the Lord.* — HEBREWS 12:14

741. *Looking diligently lest any man fail of the grace of God; lest any root of bitterness springing up trouble you, and thereby many be defiled.* — HEBREWS 12:15

I can live free from bitterness because. . .

....

....

....

....

....

....

....

....

....

....

....

....

....

....

....

742. Justice and judgment are the habitation of thy throne: mercy and truth shall go before thy face. — PSALM 89:14

743. Dearly beloved, avenge not yourselves, but rather give place unto wrath: for it is written, Vengeance is mine; I will repay, saith the Lord. — ROMANS 12:19

744. Not rendering evil for evil, or railing for railing: but contrariwise blessing; knowing that ye are thereunto called, that ye should inherit a blessing. — 1 PETER 3:9

When I am falsely accused, I will. . .

....

....

....

....

....

....

....

....

....

....

....

....

....

....

....

745. *Wherefore he saith, Awake thou that sleepest, and arise from the dead, and Christ shall give thee light.* — EPHESIANS 5:14

746. *Let thine eyes look right on, and let thine eyelids look straight before thee.* — PROVERBS 4:25

747. *I have more understanding than all my teachers: for thy testimonies are my meditation.* — PSALM 119:99

When distractions are pulling at me, I can remain focused by. . .

748. *Suffer little children to come unto me, and forbid them not: for of such is the kingdom of God. Verily I say unto you, Whosoever shall not receive the kingdom of God as a little child shall in no wise enter therein.*
— Luke 18:16–17

749. *Children's children are the crown of old men; and the glory of children are their fathers.* — Proverbs 17:6

750. *How excellent is thy lovingkindness, O God! therefore the children of men put their trust under the shadow of thy wings.* — Psalm 36:7

As I pray for the children in my life, I believe God will. . .

751. *Ye have known him that is from the beginning. . . . Ye have overcome the wicked one. . . . Ye have known the Father.* — 1 JOHN 2:13

752. *Many are the afflictions of the righteous: but the LORD delivereth him out of them all.* — PSALM 34:19

753. *These things I have spoken unto you, that in me ye might have peace. In the world ye shall have tribulation: but be of good cheer; I have overcome the world.* — JOHN 16:33

In times of trouble, God will calm my anxious heart because. . .

754. *Two are better than one; because they have a good reward for their labour. For if they fall, the one will lift up his fellow: but woe to him that is alone when he falleth; for he hath not another to help him up.*
— ECCLESIASTES 4:9–10

755. *This is my commandment, That ye love one another, as I have loved you. Greater love hath no man than this, that a man lay down his life for his friends.* — JOHN 15:12–13

756. *Ye are my friends, if ye do whatsoever I command you. Henceforth I call you not servants; for the servant knoweth not what his lord doeth: but I have called you friends; for all things that I have heard of my Father I have made known unto you.* — JOHN 15:14–15

When I think about the friends God has placed in my life. . .

....

....

....

....

....

....

....

....

....

....

....

....

757. In every thing give thanks: for this is the will of God in Christ Jesus concerning you. — 1 THESSALONIANS 5:18

758. O give thanks unto the LORD; for he is good: because his mercy endureth for ever. — PSALM 118:1

759. The blessing of the LORD, it maketh rich, and he addeth no sorrow with it. — PROVERBS 10:22

I am forever grateful for these things. . .

760. *And why beholdest thou the mote that is in thy brother's eye, but considerest not the beam that is in thine own eye?* — MATTHEW 7:3

761. *He that covereth his sins shall not prosper: but whoso confesseth and forsaketh them shall have mercy.* — PROVERBS 28:13

762. *Therefore thou art inexcusable, O man, whosoever thou art that judgest: for wherein thou judgest another, thou condemnest thyself; for thou that judgest doest the same things.* — ROMANS 2:1

When I am tempted to blame others for my failures, God's Word reminds me. . .

....

....

....

....

....

....

....

....

....

....

....

....

....

....

763. *For I reckon that the sufferings of this present time are not worthy to be compared with the glory which shall be revealed in us.* — ROMANS 8:18

764. *This is the day which the LORD hath made; we will rejoice and be glad in it.* — PSALM 118:24

765. *Let all those that seek thee rejoice and be glad in thee: let such as love thy salvation say continually, The LORD be magnified.* — PSALM 40:16

When I have a bad day, this is my prayer...

....
....
....
....
....
....
....
....
....
....
....
....
....
....
....

766. *Moreover if thy brother shall trespass against thee, go and tell him his fault between thee and him alone: if he shall hear thee, thou hast gained thy brother.* — MATTHEW 18:15

767. *And blessed is he, whosoever shall not be offended in me.* — LUKE 7:23

768. *Blessed is he whose transgression is forgiven, whose sin is covered.* — PSALM 32:1

When others offend me, I will. . .

....
....
....
....
....
....
....
....
....
....
....
....
....
....
....
....
....
....

769. *Make no friendship with an angry man; and with a furious man thou shalt not go.* — PROVERBS 22:24

770. *And whosoever shall offend one of these little ones that believe in me, it is better for him that a millstone were hanged about his neck, and he were cast into the sea.* — MARK 9:42

771. *Salt is good: but if the salt have lost his saltness, wherewith will ye season it? Have salt in yourselves, and have peace one with another.* — MARK 9:50

God gives guidance for healthy boundaries in relationships, including. . .

....

....

....

....

....

....

....

....

....

....

....

....

....

....

....

772. *So then every one of us shall give account of himself to God.*
— Romans 14:12

773. *Beware lest any man spoil you through philosophy and vain deceit, after the tradition of men, after the rudiments of the world, and not after Christ.*
— Colossians 2:8

774. *The soul that sinneth, it shall die. The son shall not bear the iniquity of the father, neither shall the father bear the iniquity of the son.*
— Ezekiel 18:20

When I think about taking responsibility for my own actions, I feel. . .

....

....

....

....

....

....

....

....

....

....

....

....

....

....

....

775. *For the love of money is the root of all evil.* — 1 Timothy 6:10

776. *Owe no man any thing, but to love one another: for he that loveth another hath fulfilled the law.* — Romans 13:8

777. *He shall lend to thee, and thou shalt not lend to him: he shall be the head, and thou shalt be the tail.* — Deuteronomy 28:44

My thoughts about accruing debt are. . .

....

....

....

....

....

....

....

....

....

....

....

....

....

....

....

....

....

778. *For I am persuaded, that neither death, nor life, nor angels, nor principalities, nor powers. . .shall be able to separate us from the love of God, which is in Christ Jesus our Lord.* — ROMANS 8:38–39

779. *If ye then be risen with Christ, seek those things which are above, where Christ sitteth on the right hand of God.* — COLOSSIANS 3:1

780. *I will ransom them from the power of the grave; I will redeem them from death.* — HOSEA 13:14

Nothing can separate me from the love of God because. . .

781. Is it not to deal thy bread to the hungry, and that thou bring the poor that are cast out to thy house? when thou seest the naked, that thou cover him? — ISAIAH 58:7

782. Now as touching things offered unto idols, we know that we all have knowledge. Knowledge puffeth up, but charity edifieth. — 1 CORINTHIANS 8:1

783. And now abideth faith, hope, charity, these three; but the greatest of these is charity. — 1 CORINTHIANS 13:13

My heart should be more charitable to others because. . .

....

....

....

....

....

....

....

....

....

....

....

....

....

....

....

784. *Thine, O LORD is the greatness, and the power, and the glory, and the victory, and the majesty: for all that is in the heaven and in the earth is thine; thine is the kingdom, O LORD, and thou art exalted as head above all.*
— 1 CHRONICLES 29:11

785. *I can do all things through Christ which strengtheneth me.*
— PHILIPPIANS 4:13

786. *The LORD shall cause thine enemies that rise up against thee to be smitten before thy face: they shall come out against thee one way, and flee before thee seven ways.* — DEUTERONOMY 28:7

When I am afraid "I can't," God's Word tells me. . .

787. *Take fast hold of instruction; let her not go: keep her; for she is thy life.*
— PROVERBS 4:13

788. *O love the LORD, all ye his saints: for the LORD preserveth the faithful, and plentifully rewardeth the proud doer.* — PSALM 31:23

789. *Hold thou me up, and I shall be safe.* — PSALM 119:117

Life's challenges cause me to hold tightly to God because...

....

....

....

....

....

....

....

....

....

....

....

....

....

....

....

....

....

790. He is ever merciful, and lendeth; and his seed is blessed. — PSALM 37:26

791. He that giveth unto the poor shall not lack: but he that hideth his eyes shall have many a curse. — PROVERBS 28:27

792. He that hath a bountiful eye shall be blessed; for he giveth of his bread to the poor. — PROVERBS 22:9

I don't want to miss a single opportunity to bless others because. . .

793. *Rejoice not against me, O mine enemy: when I fall, I shall arise; when I sit in darkness, the LORD shall be a light unto me.* — MICAH 7:8

794. *For a just man falleth seven times, and riseth up again: but the wicked shall fall into mischief.* — PROVERBS 24:16

795. *Though ye have lien among the pots, yet shall ye be as the wings of a dove covered with silver, and her feathers with yellow gold.* — PSALM 68:13

When I fall, I will rise up because. . .

796. *He that believeth on me, as the scripture hath said, out of his belly shall flow rivers of living water.* — JOHN 7:38

797. *But whosoever drinketh of the water that I shall give him shall never thirst; but the water that I shall give him shall be in him a well of water springing up into everlasting life.* — JOHN 4:14

798. *But the anointing which ye have received of him abideth in you, and ye need not that any man teach you: but as the same anointing teacheth you of all things.* — 1 JOHN 2:27

I know God's power is at work in me because. . .

. . . .

. . . .

. . . .

. . . .

. . . .

. . . .

. . . .

. . . .

. . . .

. . . .

. . . .

. . . .

. . . .

799. *That thy days may be lengthened in the land which the* LORD *thy God giveth thee. For all that do such things, and all that do unrighteously, are an abomination unto the* LORD *thy God.* — DEUTERONOMY 25:15–16

800. *For God hath not called us unto uncleanness, but unto holiness.* — 1 THESSALONIANS 4:7

801. *Ye shall do no unrighteousness in judgment, in meteyard, in weight, or in measure.* — LEVITICUS 19:35

God calls us to holiness because. . .

....

....

....

....

....

....

....

....

....

....

....

....

....

....

....

....

802. *When my father and my mother forsake me, then the LORD will take me up.* — PSALM 27:10

803. *God setteth the solitary in families.* — PSALM 68:6

804. *A man that hath friends must shew himself friendly: and there is a friend that sticketh closer than a brother.* — PROVERBS 18:24

I am never really alone because God's Word says. . .

....

....

....

....

....

....

....

....

....

....

....

....

....

....

....

....

....

805. *The thoughts of the diligent tend only to plenteousness; but of every one that is hasty only to want.* — PROVERBS 21:5

806. *The way of the slothful man is as an hedge of thorns: but the way of the righteous is made plain.* — PROVERBS 15:19

807. *He that tilleth his land shall be satisfied with bread: but he that followeth vain persons is void of understanding.* — PROVERBS 12:11

The difference between rest and laziness is. . .

....

....

....

....

....

....

....

....

....

....

....

....

....

....

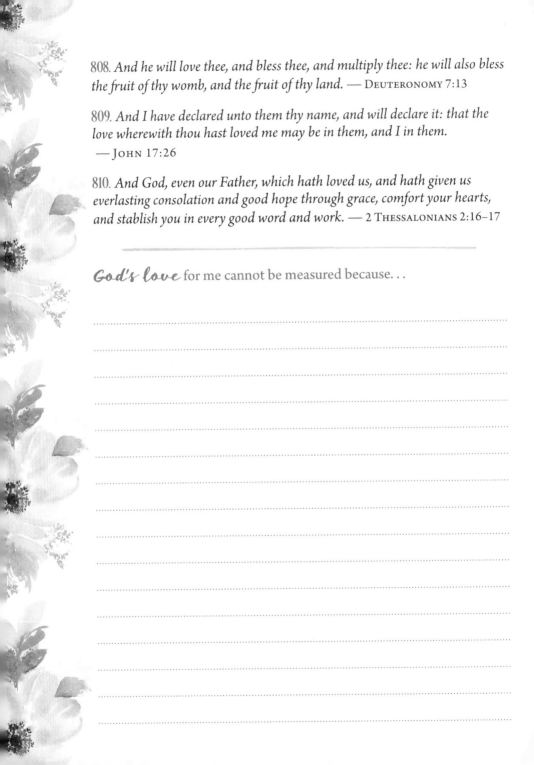

808. *And he will love thee, and bless thee, and multiply thee: he will also bless the fruit of thy womb, and the fruit of thy land.* — Deuteronomy 7:13

809. *And I have declared unto them thy name, and will declare it: that the love wherewith thou hast loved me may be in them, and I in them.* — John 17:26

810. *And God, even our Father, which hath loved us, and hath given us everlasting consolation and good hope through grace, comfort your hearts, and stablish you in every good word and work.* — 2 Thessalonians 2:16–17

God's love for me cannot be measured because. . .

811. *There is that speaketh like the piercings of a sword: but the tongue of the wise is health.* — PROVERBS 12:18

812. *But let your communication be, Yea, yea; Nay, nay: for whatsoever is more than these cometh of evil.* — MATTHEW 5:37

813. *But refuse profane and old wives' fables, and exercise thyself rather unto godliness.* — 1 TIMOTHY 4:7

When I am tempted to use my words to cause hurt, I need to remember. . .

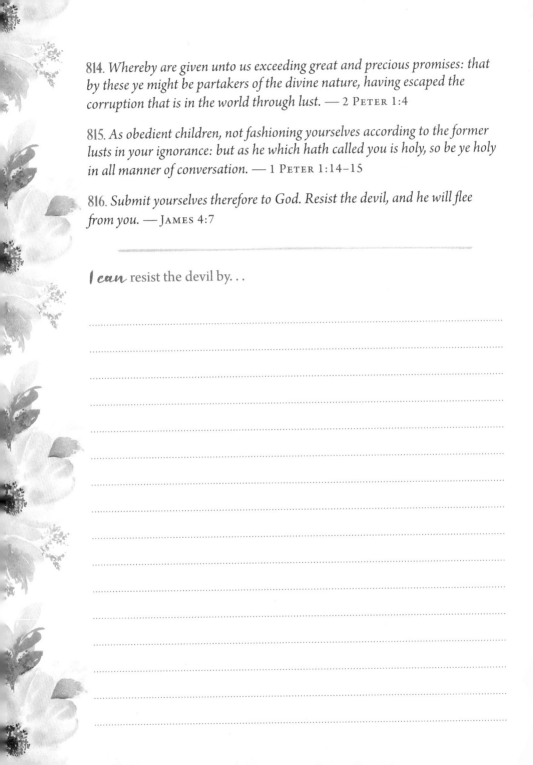

814. *Whereby are given unto us exceeding great and precious promises: that by these ye might be partakers of the divine nature, having escaped the corruption that is in the world through lust.* — 2 PETER 1:4

815. *As obedient children, not fashioning yourselves according to the former lusts in your ignorance: but as he which hath called you is holy, so be ye holy in all manner of conversation.* — 1 PETER 1:14–15

816. *Submit yourselves therefore to God. Resist the devil, and he will flee from you.* — JAMES 4:7

I can resist the devil by...

....

....

....

....

....

....

....

....

....

....

....

....

....

....

....

817. *Behold, I send an Angel before thee, to keep thee in the way, and to bring thee into the place which I have prepared.* — EXODUS 23:20

818. *And to you who are troubled rest with us, when the Lord Jesus shall be revealed from heaven with his mighty angels.* — 2 THESSALONIANS 1:7

819. *And, behold, the angel of the Lord came upon him, and a light shined in the prison: and he smote Peter on the side, and raised him up, saying, Arise up quickly. And his chains fell off from his hands.* — ACTS 12:7

When I think about the angels of the Lord assigned to me. . .

....

....

....

....

....

....

....

....

....

....

....

....

....

....

820. *To appoint unto them that mourn in Zion, to give unto them beauty for ashes, the oil of joy for mourning, the garment of praise for the spirit of heaviness.* — Isaiah 61:3

821. *Who comforteth us in all our tribulation, that we may be able to comfort them which are in any trouble, by the comfort wherewith we ourselves are comforted of God.* — 2 Corinthians 1:4

822. *Nevertheless God, that comforteth those that are cast down, comforted us.* — 2 Corinthians 7:6

When I feel down or depressed, this is my prayer. . .

823. *For the vision is yet for an appointed time, but at the end it shall speak, and not lie: though it tarry, wait for it; because it will surely come, it will not tarry.* — HABAKKUK 2:3

824. *So shall my word be that goeth forth out of my mouth: it shall not return unto me void, but it shall accomplish that which I please, and it shall prosper in the thing whereto I sent it.* — ISAIAH 55:11

825. *Commit thy works unto the LORD, and thy thoughts shall be established.* — PROVERBS 16:3

God has given me a destiny and a purpose, which is. . .

....

....

....

....

....

....

....

....

....

....

....

....

826. *For we are his workmanship, created in Christ Jesus unto good works, which God hath before ordained that we should walk in them.*
— EPHESIANS 2:10

827. *Let your light so shine before men, that they may see your good works, and glorify your Father which is in heaven.* — MATTHEW 5:16

828. *In whom the god of this world hath blinded the minds of them which believe not, lest the light of the glorious gospel of Christ, who is the image of God, should shine unto them.* — 2 CORINTHIANS 4:4

My life can point others to God in many ways, including. . .

....

....

....

....

....

....

....

....

....

....

....

....

....

....

829. *Behold, I give unto you power to tread on serpents and scorpions, and over all the power of the enemy: and nothing shall by any means hurt you.* — Luke 10:19

830. *And God said, Let us make man in our image, after our likeness: and let them have dominion over. . .every creeping thing that creepeth upon the earth.* — Genesis 1:26

831. *Thou madest him to have dominion over the works of thy hands; thou hast put all things under his feet.* — Psalm 8:6

As God's child, I have authority and dominion on this earth because. . .

....

....

....

....

....

....

....

....

....

....

....

....

....

....

....

832. *There is neither Jew nor Greek, there is neither bond nor free, there is neither male nor female: for ye are all one in Christ Jesus.* — GALATIANS 3:28

833. *For there is no respect of persons with God.* — ROMANS 2:11

834. *For all the law is fulfilled in one word, even in this; Thou shalt love thy neighbour as thyself.* — GALATIANS 5:14

In the face of discrimination, I will. . .

835. *Dearly beloved, avenge not yourselves, but rather give place unto wrath: for it is written, Vengeance is mine; I will repay, saith the Lord.* — ROMANS 12:19

836. *Then said Jesus unto him, Put up again thy sword into his place: for all they that take the sword shall perish with the sword.* — MATTHEW 26:52

837. *When the enemy shall come in like a flood, the Spirit of the LORD shall lift up a standard against him.* — ISAIAH 59:19

When things make me feel defensive, I will remember. . .

....
....
....
....
....
....
....
....
....
....
....
....
....
....
....

838. *Now I beseech you, brethren, mark them which cause divisions and offences contrary to the doctrine which ye have learned; and avoid them.* — ROMANS 16:17

839. *But avoid foolish questions, and genealogies, and contentions, and strivings about the law; for they are unprofitable and vain.* — TITUS 3:9

840. *But he, knowing their thoughts, said unto them, Every kingdom divided against itself is brought to desolation; and a house divided against a house falleth.* — LUKE 11:17

When divisions arise, this is my prayer. . .

841. *But I say unto you, That whosoever is angry with his brother without a cause shall be in danger of the judgment.* — MATTHEW 5:22

842. *But now ye also put off all these; anger, wrath, malice, blasphemy, filthy communication out of your mouth.* — COLOSSIANS 3:8

843. *Turn us, O God of our salvation, and cause thine anger toward us to cease.* — PSALM 85:4

Letting my anger get the best of me is dangerous because. . .

....

....

....

....

....

....

....

....

....

....

....

....

....

....

....

844. *And Moses said unto the LORD, O my LORD, I am not eloquent, neither heretofore, nor since thou hast spoken unto thy servant: but I am slow of speech, and of a slow tongue.* — EXODUS 4:10

845. *And the LORD God said unto the woman, What is this that thou hast done? And the woman said, The serpent beguiled me, and I did eat.* — GENESIS 3:13

846. *Neither is there any creature that is not manifest in [God's] sight: but all things are naked and opened unto the eyes of him with whom we have to do.* — HEBREWS 4:13

When I make excuses, I think God feels. . .

....

....

....

....

....

....

....

....

....

....

....

....

....

....

847. *And the man said, The woman whom thou gavest to be with me, she gave me of the tree, and I did eat.* — Genesis 3:12

848. *And Moses answered and said, But, behold, they will not believe me, nor hearken unto my voice: for they will say, The Lord hath not appeared unto thee.* — Exodus 4:1

849. *But the Lord said unto me, Say not, I am a child: for thou shalt go to all that I shall send thee, and whatsoever I command thee thou shalt speak.* — Jeremiah 1:7

When others make excuses, it makes me feel. . .

850. *For bodily exercise profiteth little: but godliness is profitable unto all things, having promise of the life that now is, and of that which is to come.*
— 1 TIMOTHY 4:8

851. *What? know ye not that your body is the temple of the Holy Ghost which is in you, which ye have of God, and ye are not your own?*
— 1 CORINTHIANS 6:19

852. *She girdeth her loins with strength, and strengtheneth her arms.*
— PROVERBS 31:17

Exercise is important because. . .

....
....
....
....
....
....
....
....
....
....
....
....
....
....
....
....

853. *When I remember these things, I pour out my soul in me: for I had gone with the multitude, I went with them to the house of God, with the voice of joy and praise, with a multitude that kept holyday.* — Psalm 42:4

854. *Hitherto have ye asked nothing in my name: ask, and ye shall receive, that your joy may be full.* — John 16:24

855. *In whom also we have obtained an inheritance, being predestinated according to the purpose of him who worketh all things after the counsel of his own will.* — Ephesians 1:11

Trusting God brings joy to my life because...

....

....

....

....

....

....

....

....

....

....

....

....

....

....

856. *I call heaven and earth to record this day against you, that I have set before you life and death, blessing and cursing: therefore choose life, that both thou and thy seed may live.* — Deuteronomy 30:19

857. *Let no man say when he is tempted, I am tempted of God: for God cannot be tempted with evil, neither tempteth he any man.* — James 1:13

858. *And that they may recover themselves out of the snare of the devil, who are taken captive by him at his will.* — 2 Timothy 2:26

God gave me the gift of free will, so I will make choices according to. . .

....

....

....

....

....

....

....

....

....

....

....

....

....

....

859. And they went forth, and preached every where, the Lord working with them, and confirming the word with signs following. Amen. — MARK 16:20

860. The same came to Jesus by night, and said unto him, Rabbi, we know that thou art a teacher come from God: for no man can do these miracles that thou doest, except God be with him. — JOHN 3:2

861. Long time therefore abode they speaking boldly in the Lord, which gave testimony unto the word of his grace, and granted signs and wonders to be done by their hands. — ACTS 14:3

The miracles God has worked in my life are. . .

....

....

....

....

....

....

....

....

....

....

....

....

....

....

862. *The beginning of strife is as when one letteth out water: therefore leave off contention, before it be meddled with.* — PROVERBS 17:14

863. *If we live in the Spirit, let us also walk in the Spirit.* — GALATIANS 5:25

864. *Having a form of godliness, but denying the power thereof: from such turn away.* — 2 TIMOTHY 3:5

When choosing to look on the positive side, I find that. . .

....

....

....

....

....

....

....

....

....

....

....

....

....

....

....

....

865. *For as the heavens are higher than the earth, so are my ways higher than your ways, and my thoughts than your thoughts.* — ISAIAH 55:9

866. *From henceforth let no man trouble me: for I bear in my body the marks of the Lord Jesus.* — GALATIANS 6:17

867. *Wherefore let them that suffer according to the will of God commit the keeping of their souls to him in well doing, as unto a faithful Creator.* — 1 PETER 4:19

When I'm nervous, I think about. . .

868. *Behold, I will do a new thing; now it shall spring forth; shall ye not know it? I will even make a way in the wilderness, and rivers in the desert.* — ISAIAH 43:19

869. *O sing unto the LORD a new song; for he hath done marvellous things: his right hand, and his holy arm, hath gotten him the victory.* — PSALM 98:1

870. *Behold, the former things are come to pass, and new things do I declare: before they spring forth I tell you of them.* — ISAIAH 42:9

God is a source of refreshment and renewal for a weary life because. . .

....

....

....

....

....

....

....

....

....

....

....

....

....

....

....

....

....

871. *The LORD, before whom I walk, will send his angel with thee, and prosper thy way.* — GENESIS 24:40

872. *And we know that all things work together for good to them that love God, to them who are the called according to his purpose.* — ROMANS 8:28

873. *The LORD is my shepherd; I shall not want.* — PSALM 23:1

When I think about God's desire to prosper me, I feel. . .

....

....

....

....

....

....

....

....

....

....

....

....

....

....

....

....

....

....

....

....

874. *And I charged your judges at that time, saying, Hear the causes between your brethren, and judge righteously between every man and his brother, and the stranger that is with him.* — DEUTERONOMY 1:16

875. *Are ye not then partial in yourselves, and are become judges of evil thoughts?* — JAMES 2:4

876. *I charge thee before God, and the Lord Jesus Christ, and the elect angels, that thou observe these things without preferring one before another, doing nothing by partiality.* — 1 TIMOTHY 5:21

When I'm tempted to judge others. . .

....
....
....
....
....
....
....
....
....
....
....
....
....
....

877. *Give her of the fruit of her hands; and let her own works praise her in the gates.* — Proverbs 31:31

878. *I must work the works of him that sent me, while it is day: the night cometh, when no man can work.* — John 9:4

879. *The hand of the diligent shall bear rule: but the slothful shall be under tribute.* — Proverbs 12:24

When I'm tempted to procrastinate, I recall that God's Word says. . .

....

....

....

....

....

....

....

....

....

....

....

....

....

....

....

880. *Most men will proclaim every one his own goodness: but a faithful man who can find?* — PROVERBS 20:6

881. *For all have sinned, and come short of the glory of God.* — ROMANS 3:23

882. *Judge not, that ye be not judged. For with what judgment ye judge, ye shall be judged: and with what measure ye mete, it shall be measured to you again.* — MATTHEW 7:1–2

On my own, I am not worthy, but because of Jesus. . .

....
....
....
....
....
....
....
....
....
....
....
....
....
....
....
....

883. *Flee fornication. Every sin that a man doeth is without the body; but he that committeth fornication sinneth against his own body.*
— 1 CORINTHIANS 6:18

884. *I say therefore to the unmarried and widows, it is good for them if they abide even as I. But if they cannot contain, let them marry: for it is better to marry than to burn.* — 1 CORINTHIANS 7:8–9

885. *Flee also youthful lusts: but follow righteousness, faith, charity, peace, with them that call on the Lord out of a pure heart.* — 2 TIMOTHY 2:22

God wants me to have a pure heart because. . .

....

....

....

....

....

....

....

....

....

....

....

....

....

....

....

886. *Turn away mine eyes from beholding vanity; and quicken thou me in thy way.* — PSALM 119:37

887. *And we know that we are of God, and the whole world lieth in wickedness.* — 1 JOHN 5:19

888. *Blessed are the pure in heart: for they shall see God.* — MATTHEW 5:8

As I consider the forms of entertainment I allow into my life, I think. . .

889. *The LORD God of your fathers make you a thousand times so many more as ye are, and bless you, as he hath promised you!* — DEUTERONOMY 1:11

890. *And now, O Lord GOD, thou art that God, and thy words be true, and thou hast promised this goodness unto thy servant.* — 2 SAMUEL 7:28

891. *The preparations of the heart in man, and the answer of the tongue, is from the LORD.* — PROVERBS 16:1

When I consider God's personal promises to me, I feel. . .

....

....

....

....

....

....

....

....

....

....

....

....

....

....

....

....

....

....

892. *Ye are the light of the world. A city that is set on an hill cannot be hid.*
— MATTHEW 5:14

893. *And every one that hath forsaken houses, or brethren, or sisters, or father, or mother, or wife, or children, or lands, for my name's sake, shall receive an hundredfold, and shall inherit everlasting life.* — MATTHEW 19:29

894. *Nevertheless we, according to his promise, look for new heavens and a new earth, wherein dwelleth righteousness.* — 2 PETER 3:13

I want to make a positive difference in the lives of others, so I will. . .

895. *Nay, in all these things we are more than conquerors through him that loved us.* — ROMANS 8:37

896. *But thanks be to God, which giveth us the victory through our Lord Jesus Christ.* — 1 CORINTHIANS 15:57

897. *And I saw, and behold a white horse: and he that sat on him had a bow; and a crown was given unto him: and he went forth conquering, and to conquer.* — REVELATION 6:2

I am more than a conqueror because. . .

....

....

....

....

....

....

....

....

....

....

....

....

....

....

....

898. *Whether therefore ye eat, or drink, or whatsoever ye do, do all to the glory of God.* — 1 CORINTHIANS 10:31

899. *Redeeming the time, because the days are evil.* — EPHESIANS 5:16

900. *To every thing there is a season, and a time to every purpose under the heaven. . .a time to weep, and a time to laugh; a time to mourn, and a time to dance.* — ECCLESIASTES 3:1, 4

God's Word helps me to prioritize by. . .

901. *The* Lord *said unto Samuel. . .the* Lord *seeth not as man seeth; for man looketh on the outward appearance, but the* Lord *looketh on the heart.* — 1 Samuel 16:7

902. *Favour is deceitful, and beauty is vain: but a woman that feareth the* Lord, *she shall be praised.* — Proverbs 31:30

903. *As a jewel of gold in a swine's snout, so is a fair woman which is without discretion.* — Proverbs 11:22

Appearances mean little, because God's Word says. . .

....

....

....

....

....

....

....

....

....

....

....

....

....

....

904. *And he believed in the Lord; and he counted it to him for righteousness.* — GENESIS 15:6

905. *The Lord shall judge the people: judge me, O Lord, according to my righteousness, and according to mine integrity that is in me.* — PSALM 7:8

906. *Him that is weak in the faith receive ye, but not to doubtful disputations.* — ROMANS 14:1

When I consider the opinions of others, I. . .

....
....
....
....
....
....
....
....
....
....
....
....
....
....
....
....
....

907. *Let all things be done decently and in order.* — 1 Corinthians 14:40

908. *For God is not the author of confusion, but of peace, as in all churches of the saints.* — 1 Corinthians 14:33

909. *For by him were all things created, that are in heaven, and that are in earth, visible and invisible, whether they be thrones, or dominions, or principalities, or powers: all things were created by him.* — Colossians 1:16

I am so thankful God is the author of peace and order because. . .

. . . .

. . . .

. . . .

. . . .

. . . .

. . . .

. . . .

. . . .

. . . .

. . . .

. . . .

. . . .

. . . .

. . . .

910. *For our heart shall rejoice in him, because we have trusted in his holy name.* — PSALM 33:21

911. *I will see you again, and your heart shall rejoice, and your joy no man taketh from you.* — JOHN 16:22

912. *The righteous shall be glad in the LORD, and shall trust in him; and all the upright in heart shall glory.* — PSALM 64:10

I won't let anyone steal my joy because. . .

913. *What shall we then say to these things? If God be for us, who can be against us?* — ROMANS 8:31

914. *Surely he hath borne our griefs, and carried our sorrows: yet we did esteem him stricken, smitten of God, and afflicted.* — ISAIAH 53:4

915. *But as for me, my prayer is unto thee, O LORD, in an acceptable time: O God, in the multitude of thy mercy hear me, in the truth of thy salvation.* — PSALM 69:13

When I feel the sting of rejection, I find comfort in. . .

916. *There is therefore now no condemnation to them which are in Christ Jesus, who walk not after the flesh, but after the Spirit.* — ROMANS 8:1

917. *And ye shall know the truth, and the truth shall make you free.* — JOHN 8:32

918. *Above all, taking the shield of faith, wherewith ye shall be able to quench all the fiery darts of the wicked.* — EPHESIANS 6:16

Sometimes I feel insecure because. . .

....

....

....

....

....

....

....

....

....

....

....

....

....

....

....

....

....

919. *As many as I love, I rebuke and chasten: be zealous therefore, and repent.*
— Revelation 3:19

920. *For I bear them record that they have a zeal of God, but not according to knowledge.* — Romans 10:2

921. *Who gave himself for us, that he might redeem us from all iniquity, and purify unto himself a peculiar people, zealous of good works.* — Titus 2:14

A personal relationship with Jesus Christ means. . .

....
....
....
....
....
....
....
....
....
....
....
....
....
....

922. *A good man out of the good treasure of the heart bringeth forth good things: and an evil man out of the evil treasure bringeth forth evil things.*
— MATTHEW 12:35

923. *Jesus said unto him, Thou shalt love the Lord thy God with all thy heart, and with all thy soul, and with all thy mind.* — MATTHEW 22:37

924. *My son, attend to my words; incline thine ear unto my sayings. For they are life unto those that find them, and health to all their flesh.*
— PROVERBS 4:20, 22

I will always guard my heart because. . .

925. *My covenant will I not break, nor alter the thing that is gone out of my lips.* — PSALM 89:34

926. *And also the Strength of Israel will not lie nor repent: for he is not a man, that he should repent.* — 1 SAMUEL 15:29

927. *For all the promises of God in him are yea, and in him Amen, unto the glory of God by us.* — 2 CORINTHIANS 1:20

I show my thankfulness to God by. . .

....

....

....

....

....

....

....

....

....

....

....

....

....

....

928. *And the Lord shall deliver me from every evil work, and will preserve me unto his heavenly kingdom: to whom be glory for ever and ever. Amen.*
— 2 Timothy 4:18

929. *Teaching them to observe all things whatsoever I have commanded you: and, lo, I am with you always, even unto the end of the world. Amen.*
— Matthew 28:20

930. *Shew thy marvellous lovingkindness, O thou that savest by thy right hand them which put their trust in thee from those that rise up against them.*
— Psalm 17:7

When I call on God to keep me, deliver me, and save me, He. . .

931. *He restoreth my soul: he leadeth me in the paths of righteousness for his name's sake.* — PSALM 23:3

932. *For what shall it profit a man, if he shall gain the whole world, and lose his own soul?* — MARK 8:36

933. *Shew me thy ways, O LORD; teach me thy paths. Lead me in thy truth, and teach me: for thou art the God of my salvation; on thee do I wait all the day.* - — PSALM 25:4–5

When my soul stops to listen to God. . .

....

....

....

....

....

....

....

....

....

....

....

....

....

....

....

934. *The LORD is good unto them that wait for him, to the soul that seeketh him.* — LAMENTATIONS 3:25

935. *Our soul waiteth for the LORD: he is our help and our shield. For our heart shall rejoice in him, because we have trusted in his holy name.* — PSALM 33:20–21

936. *Behold, we count them happy which endure. Ye have heard of the patience of Job, and have seen the end of the Lord; that the Lord is very pitiful, and of tender mercy.* — JAMES 5:11

When I wait patiently on the Lord. . .

937. *Behold, what manner of love the Father hath bestowed upon us, that we should be called the sons of God: therefore the world knoweth us not, because it knew him not.* — 1 JOHN 3:1

938. *Ye are of God, little children, and have overcome them: because greater is he that is in you, than he that is in the world.* — 1 JOHN 4:4

939. *But ye are a chosen generation, a royal priesthood, an holy nation, a peculiar people; that ye should shew forth the praises of him who hath called you out of darkness into his marvellous light.* — 1 PETER 2:9

Because of Christ, I am...

940. *And ye shall hear of wars and rumours of wars: see that ye be not troubled: for all these things must come to pass, but the end is not yet.*
— MATTHEW 24:6

941. *Persecutions, afflictions, which came unto me at Antioch, at Iconium, at Lystra; what persecutions I endured: but out of them all the Lord delivered me.* — 2 TIMOTHY 3:11

942. *Declaring the end from the beginning, and from ancient times the things that are not yet done, saying, My counsel shall stand, and I will do all my pleasure.* — ISAIAH 46:10

Though the world may be falling apart around me, I have hope because. . .

943. *Till he fill thy mouth with laughing, and thy lips with rejoicing.* — JOB 8:21

944. *Then was our mouth filled with laughter, and our tongue with singing: then said they among the heathen, The LORD hath done great things for them.* — PSALM 126:2

945. *Blessed are ye that hunger now: for ye shall be filled. Blessed are ye that weep now: for ye shall laugh.* — LUKE 6:21

I am thankful for the gift of laughter, because it makes me. . .

946. *Hast thou not known? hast thou not heard, that the everlasting God, the LORD, the Creator of the ends of the earth, fainteth not, neither is weary? there is no searching of his understanding.* — ISAIAH 40:28

947. *When I consider thy heavens, the work of thy fingers, the moon and the stars, which thou hast ordained; what is man, that thou art mindful of him? and the son of man, that thou visitest him?* — PSALM 8:3–4

948. *Before I formed thee in the belly I knew thee; and before thou camest forth out of the womb I sanctified thee, and I ordained thee a prophet unto the nations.* — JEREMIAH 1:5

I need never place limits on God because. . .

....
....
....
....
....
....
....
....
....
....
....
....
....
....
....

949. *It is a sign between me and the children of Israel for ever: for in six days the LORD made heaven and earth, and on the seventh day he rested, and was refreshed.* — EXODUS 31:17

950. *For thus saith the high and lofty One that inhabiteth eternity, whose name is Holy; I dwell in the high and holy place, with him also that is of a contrite and humble spirit, to revive the spirit of the humble, and to revive the heart of the contrite ones.* — ISAIAH 57:15

951. *The humble shall see this, and be glad: and your heart shall live that seek God.* — PSALM 69:32

When I need a spiritual refreshing, this is my prayer. . .

....

....

....

....

....

....

....

....

....

....

....

....

....

....

952. *And looking round about upon them all, he said unto the man, Stretch forth thy hand. And he did so: and his hand was restored whole as the other.* — LUKE 6:10

953. *And he said unto her, Daughter, thy faith hath made thee whole; go in peace, and be whole of thy plague.* — MARK 5:34

954. *And Peter answered him and said, Lord, if it be thou, bid me come unto thee on the water. And he said, Come. And when Peter was come down out of the ship, he walked on the water, to go to Jesus.* — MATTHEW 14:28–29

Reading the stories of miracles in the Bible sparks my faith because. . .

....

....

....

....

....

....

....

....

....

....

....

....

....

....

955. *The redeemed of the LORD shall return, and come with singing unto Zion; and everlasting joy shall be upon their head: they shall obtain gladness and joy; and sorrow and mourning shall flee away.* — ISAIAH 51:11

956. *I will greatly rejoice in the LORD, my soul shall be joyful in my God; for he hath clothed me with the garments of salvation.* — ISAIAH 61:10

957. *For this day is holy unto our LORD: neither be ye sorry; for the joy of the LORD is your strength.* — NEHEMIAH 8:10

Even in difficult times, my heart can overflow with joy because I know. . .

....

....

....

....

....

....

....

....

....

....

....

....

....

958. *Ointment and perfume rejoice the heart: so doth the sweetness of a man's friend by hearty counsel.* — PROVERBS 27:9

959. *Where no counsel is, the people fall: but in the multitude of counsellors there is safety.* — PROVERBS 11:14

960. *And Ruth said, Intreat me not to leave thee, or to return from following after thee: for whither thou goest, I will go; and where thou lodgest, I will lodge: thy people shall be my people, and thy God my God.* — RUTH 1:16

The friendships that mean the most to me. . .

....

....

....

....

....

....

....

....

....

....

....

....

....

....

....

961. *But these are written, that ye might believe that Jesus is the Christ, the Son of God; and that believing ye might have life through his name.* — JOHN 20:31

962. *Truly the signs of an apostle were wrought among you in all patience, in signs, and wonders, and mighty deeds.* — 2 CORINTHIANS 12:12

963. *God also bearing them witness, both with signs and wonders, and with divers miracles, and gifts of the Holy Ghost, according to his own will?* — HEBREWS 2:4

I know God still works miracles today because. . .

....

....

....

....

....

....

....

....

....

....

....

....

....

....

....

964. *But he giveth more grace. Wherefore he saith, God resisteth the proud, but giveth grace unto the humble.* — JAMES 4:6

965. *Whosoever therefore shall humble himself as this little child, the same is greatest in the kingdom of heaven.* — MATTHEW 18:4

966. *Better it is to be of an humble spirit with the lowly, than to divide the spoil with the proud.* — PROVERBS 16:19

When I give God the credit for my accomplishments, this shows others that. . .

967. The LORD shall fight for you, and ye shall hold your peace.
— Exodus 14:14

968. The LORD will give strength unto his people; the LORD will bless his people with peace. — Psalm 29:11

969. He that is void of wisdom despiseth his neighbour: but a man of understanding holdeth his peace. — Proverbs 11:12

Anger doesn't benefit me or others because. . .

970. *Now the just shall live by faith: but if any man draw back, my soul shall have no pleasure in him.* — HEBREWS 10:38

971. *But strong meat belongeth to them that are of full age, even those who by reason of use have their senses exercised to discern both good and evil.* — HEBREWS 5:14

972. *For the word of the LORD is right; and all his works are done in truth.* — PSALM 33:4

When my faith is challenged, I will. . .

....

....

....

....

....

....

....

....

....

....

....

....

....

....

....

....

973. *Yea, in the way of thy judgments, O Lord, have we waited for thee; the desire of our soul is to thy name, and to the remembrance of thee.*
— Isaiah 26:8

974. *Thou wilt say then unto me, Why doth he yet find fault? For who hath resisted his will?* — Romans 9:19

975. *Without counsel purposes are disappointed: but in the multitude of counsellors they are established.* — Proverbs 15:22

When I need decision-making guidance, the best advice always comes from. . .

....

....

....

....

....

....

....

....

....

....

....

....

....

....

....

976. *To have respect of persons is not good: for for a piece of bread that man will transgress.* — PROVERBS 28:21

977. *But the wisdom that is from above is first pure, then peaceable, gentle, and easy to be intreated, full of mercy and good fruits, without partiality, and without hypocrisy.* — JAMES 3:17

978. *But in every nation he that feareth him, and worketh righteousness, is accepted with him.* — ACTS 10:35

I show respect to others by. . .

....

....

....

....

....

....

....

....

....

....

....

....

....

....

....

....

979. *Praying always with all prayer and supplication in the Spirit, and watching thereunto with all perseverance and supplication for all saints.*
— Ephesians 6:18

980. *I will therefore that men pray every where, lifting up holy hands, without wrath and doubting.* — 1 Timothy 2:8

981. *I have called upon thee, for thou wilt hear me, O God: incline thine ear unto me, and hear my speech.* — Psalm 17:6

My prayer life on a scale of strong (10) to weak (1) is. . .

982. *Faithful are the wounds of a friend; but the kisses of an enemy are deceitful.* — PROVERBS 27:6

983. *The righteous is more excellent than his neighbour: but the way of the wicked seduceth them.* — PROVERBS 12:26

984. *He that covereth a transgression seeketh love; but he that repeateth a matter separateth very friends.* — PROVERBS 17:9

"Faithful are the wounds of a friend" means. . .

....

....

....

....

....

....

....

....

....

....

....

....

....

....

....

....

985. *And God called the firmament Heaven. And the evening and the morning were the second day.* — GENESIS 1:8

986. *Know therefore this day, and consider it in thine heart, that the LORD he is God in heaven above, and upon the earth beneath: there is none else.* — DEUTERONOMY 4:39

987. *And I heard a voice from heaven, as the voice of many waters, and as the voice of a great thunder: and I heard the voice of harpers harping with their harps.* — REVELATION 14:2

I know heaven is real because. . .

....

....

....

....

....

....

....

....

....

....

....

....

....

....

988. Precious in the sight of the LORD is the death of his saints.
— PSALM 116:15

989. Mark the perfect man, and behold the upright: for the end of that man is peace. — PSALM 37:37

990. He will swallow up death in victory; and the Lord GOD will wipe away tears from off all faces. — ISAIAH 25:8

Death is never victorious in the lives of Christ followers because. . .

....

....

....

....

....

....

....

....

....

....

....

....

....

....

....

....

991. *When thou passest through the waters, I will be with thee; and through the rivers, they shall not overflow thee: when thou walkest through the fire, thou shalt not be burned.* — Isaiah 43:2

992. *Peace I leave with you, my peace I give unto you: not as the world giveth, give I unto you. Let not your heart be troubled, neither let it be afraid.* — John 14:27

993. *And fear not them which kill the body, but are not able to kill the soul.* — Matthew 10:28

I will refuse to give in to fear because. . .

....

....

....

....

....

....

....

....

....

....

....

....

....

....

994. *And this is the record, that God hath given to us eternal life, and this life is in his Son.* — 1 JOHN 5:11

995. *But is now made manifest by the appearing of our Saviour Jesus Christ, who hath abolished death, and hath brought life and immortality to light through the gospel.* — 2 TIMOTHY 1:10

996. *Jesus said unto her, I am the resurrection, and the life: he that believeth in me, though he were dead, yet shall he live.* — JOHN 11:25

I am thankful for the gift of eternal life because. . .

....

....

....

....

....

....

....

....

....

....

....

....

....

....

....

....

997. *And when the Lord saw her, he had compassion on her, and said unto her, Weep not.* — Luke 7:13

998. *And of some have compassion, making a difference.* — Jude 1:22

999. *Thus speaketh the Lord of hosts, saying, Execute true judgment, and shew mercy and compassions every man to his brother.* — Zechariah 7:9

When I respond to others with Christlike compassion, I feel. . .

....

....

....

....

....

....

....

....

....

....

....

....

....

....

....

....

1000. *And the hand of the Lord was with them: and a great number believed, and turned unto the Lord.* — ACTS 11:21

I want others to know Jesus like I do. Here is a list of people I'll be praying for daily. . .

....
....
....
....
....
....
....
....
....
....
....
....
....
....
....
....
....
....
....
....

READ THROUGH THE BIBLE IN A YEAR

1-Jan	Gen. 1-2	Matt. 1	Ps. 1
2-Jan	Gen. 3-4	Matt. 2	Ps. 2
3-Jan	Gen. 5-7	Matt. 3	Ps. 3
4-Jan	Gen. 8-10	Matt. 4	Ps. 4
5-Jan	Gen. 11-13	Matt. 5:1-20	Ps. 5
6-Jan	Gen. 14-16	Matt. 5:21-48	Ps. 6
7-Jan	Gen. 17-18	Matt. 6:1-18	Ps. 7
8-Jan	Gen. 19-20	Matt. 6:19-34	Ps. 8
9-Jan	Gen. 21-23	Matt. 7:1-11	Ps. 9:1-8
10-Jan	Gen. 24	Matt. 7:12-29	Ps. 9:9-20
11-Jan	Gen. 25-26	Matt. 8:1-17	Ps. 10:1-11
12-Jan	Gen. 27:1-28:9	Matt. 8:18-34	Ps. 10:12-18
13-Jan	Gen. 28:10-29:35	Matt. 9	Ps. 11
14-Jan	Gen. 30:1-31:21	Matt. 10:1-15	Ps. 12
15-Jan	Gen. 31:22-32:21	Matt. 10:16-36	Ps. 13
16-Jan	Gen. 32:22-34:31	Matt. 10:37-11:6	Ps. 14
17-Jan	Gen. 35-36	Matt. 11:7-24	Ps. 15
18-Jan	Gen. 37-38	Matt. 11:25-30	Ps. 16
19-Jan	Gen. 39-40	Matt. 12:1-29	Ps. 17
20-Jan	Gen. 41	Matt. 12:30-50	Ps. 18:1-15
21-Jan	Gen. 42-43	Matt. 13:1-9	Ps. 18:16-29
22-Jan	Gen. 44-45	Matt. 13:10-23	Ps. 18:30-50
23-Jan	Gen. 46:1-47:26	Matt. 13:24-43	Ps. 19
24-Jan	Gen. 47:27-49:28	Matt. 13:44-58	Ps. 20
25-Jan	Gen. 49:29-Exod. 1:22	Matt. 14	Ps. 21
26-Jan	Exod. 2-3	Matt. 15:1-28	Ps. 22:1-21
27-Jan	Exod. 4:1-5:21	Matt. 15:29-16:12	Ps. 22:22-31
28-Jan	Exod. 5:22-7:24	Matt. 16:13-28	Ps. 23
29-Jan	Exod. 7:25-9:35	Matt. 17:1-9	Ps. 24
30-Jan	Exod. 10-11	Matt. 17:10-27	Ps. 25
31-Jan	Exod. 12	Matt. 18:1-20	Ps. 26
1-Feb	Exod. 13-14	Matt. 18:21-35	Ps. 27
2-Feb	Exod. 15-16	Matt. 19:1-15	Ps. 28
3-Feb	Exod. 17-19	Matt. 19:16-30	Ps. 29
4-Feb	Exod. 20-21	Matt. 20:1-19	Ps. 30

5-Feb	Exod. 22-23	Matt. 20:20-34	Ps. 31:1-8
6-Feb	Exod. 24-25	Matt. 21:1-27	Ps. 31:9-18
7-Feb	Exod 26-27	Matt. 21:28-46	Ps. 31:19-24
8-Feb	Exod. 28	Matt. 22	Ps. 32
9-Feb	Exod. 29	Matt. 23:1-36	Ps. 33:1-12
10-Feb	Exod. 30-31	Matt. 23:37-24:28	Ps. 33:13-22
11-Feb	Exod. 32-33	Matt. 24:29-51	Ps. 34:1-7
12-Feb	Exod. 34:1-35:29	Matt. 25:1-13	Ps. 34:8-22
13-Feb	Exod. 35:30-37:29	Matt. 25:14-30	Ps. 35:1-8
14-Feb	Exod. 38-39	Matt. 25:31-46	Ps. 35:9-17
15-Feb	Exod. 40	Matt. 26:1-35	Ps. 35:18-28
16-Feb	Lev. 1-3	Matt. 26:36-68	Ps. 36:1-6
17-Feb	Lev. 4:1-5:13	Matt. 26:69-27:26	Ps. 36:7-12
18-Feb	Lev. 5:14 -7:21	Matt. 27:27-50	Ps. 37:1-6
19-Feb	Lev. 7:22-8:36	Matt. 27:51-66	Ps. 37:7-26
20-Feb	Lev. 9-10	Matt. 28	Ps. 37:27-40
21-Feb	Lev. 11-12	Mark 1:1-28	Ps. 38
22-Feb	Lev. 13	Mark 1:29-39	Ps. 39
23-Feb	Lev. 14	Mark 1:40-2:12	Ps. 40:1-8
24-Feb	Lev. 15	Mark 2:13-3:35	Ps. 40:9-17
25-Feb	Lev. 16-17	Mark 4:1-20	Ps. 41:1-4
26-Feb	Lev. 18-19	Mark 4:21-41	Ps. 41:5-13
27-Feb	Lev. 20	Mark 5	Ps. 42-43
28-Feb	Lev. 21-22	Mark 6:1-13	Ps. 44
1-Mar	Lev. 23-24	Mark 6:14-29	Ps. 45:1-5
2-Mar	Lev. 25	Mark 6:30-56	Ps. 45:6-12
3-Mar	Lev. 26	Mark 7	Ps. 45:13-17
4-Mar	Lev. 27	Mark 8	Ps. 46
5-Mar	Num. 1-2	Mark 9:1-13	Ps. 47
6-Mar	Num. 3	Mark 9:14-50	Ps. 48:1-8
7-Mar	Num. 4	Mark 10:1-34	Ps. 48:9-14
8-Mar	Num. 5:1-6:21	Mark 10:35-52	Ps. 49:1-9
9-Mar	Num. 6:22-7:47	Mark 11	Ps. 49:10-20
10-Mar	Num. 7:48-8:4	Mark 12:1-27	Ps. 50:1-15
11-Mar	Num. 8:5-9:23	Mark 12:28-44	Ps. 50:16-23
12-Mar	Num. 10-11	Mark 13:1-8	Ps. 51:1-9

13-Mar	Num. 12-13	Mark 13:9-37	Ps. 51:10-19
14-Mar	Num. 14	Mark 14:1-31	Ps. 52
15-Mar	Num. 15	Mark 14:32-72	Ps. 53
16-Mar	Num. 16	Mark 15:1-32	Ps. 54
17-Mar	Num. 17-18	Mark 15:33-47	Ps. 55
18-Mar	Num. 19-20	Mark 16	Ps. 56:1-7
19-Mar	Num. 21:1-22:20	Luke 1:1-25	Ps. 56:8-13
20-Mar	Num. 22:21-23:30	Luke 1:26-56	Ps. 57
21-Mar	Num. 24-25	Luke 1:57-2:20	Ps. 58
22-Mar	Num. 26:1-27:11	Luke 2:21-38	Ps. 59:1-8
23-Mar	Num. 27:12-29:11	Luke 2:39-52	Ps. 59:9-17
24-Mar	Num. 29:12-30:16	Luke 3	Ps. 60:1-5
25-Mar	Num. 31	Luke 4	Ps. 60:6-12
26-Mar	Num. 32-33	Luke 5:1-16	Ps. 61
27-Mar	Num. 34-36	Luke 5:17-32	Ps. 62:1-6
28-Mar	Deut. 1:1-2:25	Luke 5:33-6:11	Ps. 62:7-12
29-Mar	Deut. 2:26-4:14	Luke 6:12-35	Ps. 63:1-5
30-Mar	Deut. 4:15-5:22	Luke 6:36-49	Ps. 63:6-11
31-Mar	Deut. 5:23-7:26	Luke 7:1-17	Ps. 64:1-5
1-Apr	Deut. 8-9	Luke 7:18-35	Ps. 64:6-10
2-Apr	Deut. 10-11	Luke 7:36-8:3	Ps. 65:1-8
3-Apr	Deut. 12-13	Luke 8:4-21	Ps. 65:9-13
4-Apr	Deut. 14:1-16:8	Luke 8:22-39	Ps. 66:1-7
5-Apr	Deut. 16:9-18:22	Luke 8:40-56	Ps. 66:8-15
6-Apr	Deut. 19:1-21:9	Luke 9:1-22	Ps. 66:16-20
7-Apr	Deut. 21:10-23:8	Luke 9:23-42	Ps. 67
8-Apr	Deut. 23:9-25:19	Luke 9:43-62	Ps. 68:1-6
9-Apr	Deut. 26:1-28:14	Luke 10:1-20	Ps. 68:7-14
10-Apr	Deut. 28:15-68	Luke 10:21-37	Ps. 68:15-19
11-Apr	Deut. 29-30	Luke 10:38-11:23	Ps. 68:20-27
12-Apr	Deut. 31:1-32:22	Luke 11:24-36	Ps. 68:28-35
13-Apr	Deut. 32:23-33:29	Luke 11:37-54	Ps. 69:1-9
14-Apr	Deut. 34-Josh. 2	Luke 12:1-15	Ps. 69:10-17
15-Apr	Josh. 3:1-5:12	Luke 12:16-40	Ps. 69:18-28
16-Apr	Josh. 5:13-7:26	Luke 12:41-48	Ps. 69:29-36
17-Apr	Josh. 8-9	Luke 12:49-59	Ps. 70

18-APR	JOSH. 10:1-11:15	LUKE 13:1-21	PS. 71:1-6
19-APR	JOSH. 11:16-13:33	LUKE 13:22-35	PS. 71:7-16
20-APR	JOSH. 14-16	LUKE 14:1-15	PS. 71:17-21
21-APR	JOSH. 17:1-19:16	LUKE 14:16-35	PS. 71:22-24
22-APR	JOSH. 19:17-21:42	LUKE 15:1-10	PS. 72:1-11
23-APR	JOSH. 21:43-22:34	LUKE 15:11-32	PS. 72:12-20
24-APR	JOSH. 23-24	LUKE 16:1-18	PS. 73:1-9
25-APR	JUDG. 1-2	LUKE 16:19-17:10	PS. 73:10-20
26-APR	JUDG. 3-4	LUKE 17:11-37	PS. 73:21-28
27-APR	JUDG. 5:1-6:24	LUKE 18:1-17	PS. 74:1-3
28-APR	JUDG. 6:25-7:25	LUKE 18:18-43	PS. 74:4-11
29-APR	JUDG. 8:1-9:23	LUKE 19:1-28	PS. 74:12-17
30-APR	JUDG. 9:24-10:18	LUKE 19:29-48	PS. 74:18-23
1-MAY	JUDG. 11:1-12:7	LUKE 20:1-26	PS. 75:1-7
2-MAY	JUDG. 12:8-14:20	LUKE 20:27-47	PS. 75:8-10
3-MAY	JUDG. 15-16	LUKE 21:1-19	PS. 76:1-7
4-MAY	JUDG. 17-18	LUKE 21:20-22:6	PS. 76:8-12
5-MAY	JUDG. 19:1-20:23	LUKE 22:7-30	PS. 77:1-11
6-MAY	JUDG. 20:24-21:25	LUKE 22:31-54	PS. 77:12-20
7-MAY	RUTH 1-2	LUKE 22:55-23:25	PS. 78:1-4
8-MAY	RUTH 3-4	LUKE 23:26-24:12	PS. 78:5-8
9-MAY	1 SAM. 1:1-2:21	LUKE 24:13-53	PS. 78:9-16
10-MAY	1 SAM. 2:22-4:22	JOHN 1:1-28	PS. 78:17-24
11-MAY	1 SAM. 5-7	JOHN 1:29-51	PS. 78:25-33
12-MAY	1 SAM. 8:1-9:26	JOHN 2	PS. 78:34-41
13-MAY	1 SAM. 9:27-11:15	JOHN 3:1-22	PS. 78:42-55
14-MAY	1 SAM. 12-13	JOHN 3:23-4:10	PS. 78:56-66
15-MAY	1 SAM. 14	JOHN 4:11-38	PS. 78:67-72
16-MAY	1 SAM. 15-16	JOHN 4:39-54	PS. 79:1-7
17-MAY	1 SAM. 17	JOHN 5:1-24	PS. 79:8-13
18-MAY	1 SAM. 18-19	JOHN 5:25-47	PS. 80:1-7
19-MAY	1 SAM. 20-21	JOHN 6:1-21	PS. 80:8-19
20-MAY	1 SAM. 22-23	JOHN 6:22-42	PS. 81:1-10
21-MAY	1 SAM. 24:1-25:31	JOHN 6:43-71	PS. 81:11-16
22-MAY	1 SAM. 25:32-27:12	JOHN 7:1-24	PS. 82
23-MAY	1 SAM. 28-29	JOHN 7:25-8:11	PS. 83

24-May	1 Sam. 30-31	John 8:12-47	Ps. 84:1-4
25-May	2 Sam. 1-2	John 8:48-9:12	Ps. 84:5-12
26-May	2 Sam. 3-4	John 9:13-34	Ps. 85:1-7
27-May	2 Sam. 5:1-7:17	John 9:35-10:10	Ps. 85:8-13
28-May	2 Sam. 7:18-10:19	John 10:11-30	Ps. 86:1-10
29-May	2 Sam. 11:1-12:25	John 10:31-11:16	Ps. 86:11-17
30-May	2 Sam. 12:26-13:39	John 11:17-54	Ps. 87
31-May	2 Sam. 14:1-15:12	John 11:55-12:19	Ps. 88:1-9
1-Jun	2 Sam. 15:13-16:23	John 12:20-43	Ps. 88:10-18
2-Jun	2 Sam. 17:1-18:18	John 12:44-13:20	Ps. 89:1-6
3-Jun	2 Sam. 18:19-19:39	John 13:21-38	Ps. 89:7-13
4-Jun	2 Sam. 19:40-21:22	John 14:1-17	Ps. 89:14-18
5-Jun	2 Sam. 22:1-23:7	John 14:18-15:27	Ps. 89:19-29
6-Jun	2 Sam. 23:8-24:25	John 16:1-22	Ps. 89:30-37
7-Jun	1 Kings 1	John 16:23-17:5	Ps. 89:38-52
8-Jun	1 Kings 2	John 17:6-26	Ps. 90:1-12
9-Jun	1 Kings 3-4	John 18:1-27	Ps. 90:13-17
10-Jun	1 Kings 5-6	John 18:28-19:5	Ps. 91:1-10
11-Jun	1 Kings 7	John 19:6-25a	Ps. 91:11-16
12-Jun	1 Kings 8:1-53	John 19:25b-42	Ps. 92:1-9
13-Jun	1 Kings 8:54-10:13	John 20:1-18	Ps. 92:10-15
14-Jun	1 Kings 10:14-11:43	John 20:19-31	Ps. 93
15-Jun	1 Kings 12:1-13:10	John 21	Ps. 94:1-11
16-Jun	1 Kings 13:11-14:31	Acts 1:1-11	Ps. 94:12-23
17-Jun	1 Kings 15:1-16:20	Acts 1:12-26	Ps. 95
18-Jun	1 Kings 16:21-18:19	Acts 2:1-21	Ps. 96:1-8
19-Jun	1 Kings 18:20-19:21	Acts 2:22-41	Ps. 96:9-13
20-Jun	1 Kings 20	Acts 2:42-3:26	Ps. 97:1-6
21-Jun	1 Kings 21:1-22:28	Acts 4:1-22	Ps. 97:7-12
22-Jun	1 Kings 22:29- 2 Kings 1:18	Acts 4:23-5:11	Ps. 98
23-Jun	2 Kings 2-3	Acts 5:12-28	Ps. 99
24-Jun	2 Kings 4	Acts 5:29-6:15	Ps. 100
25-Jun	2 Kings 5:1-6:23	Acts 7:1-16	Ps. 101
26-Jun	2 Kings 6:24-8:15	Acts 7:17-36	Ps. 102:1-7
27-Jun	2 Kings 8:16-9:37	Acts 7:37-53	Ps. 102:8-17

28-Jun	2 Kings 10-11	Acts 7:54-8:8	Ps. 102:18-28
29-Jun	2 Kings 12-13	Acts 8:9-40	Ps. 103:1-9
30-Jun	2 Kings 14-15	Acts 9:1-16	Ps. 103:10-14
1-Jul	2 Kings 16-17	Acts 9:17-31	Ps. 103:15-22
2-Jul	2 Kings 18:1-19:7	Acts 9:32-10:16	Ps. 104:1-9
3-Jul	2 Kings 19:8-20:21	Acts 10:17-33	Ps. 104:10-23
4-Jul	2 Kings 21:1-22:20	Acts 10:34-11:18	Ps. 104: 24-30
5-Jul	2 Kings 23	Acts 11:19-12:17	Ps. 104:31-35
6-Jul	2 Kings 24-25	Acts 12:18-13:13	Ps. 105:1-7
7-Jul	1 Chron. 1-2	Acts 13:14-43	Ps. 105:8-15
8-Jul	1 Chron. 3:1-5:10	Acts 13:44-14:10	Ps. 105:16-28
9-Jul	1 Chron. 5:11-6:81	Acts 14:11-28	Ps. 105:29-36
10-Jul	1 Chron. 7:1-9:9	Acts 15:1-18	Ps. 105:37-45
11-Jul	1 Chron. 9:10-11:9	Acts 15:19-41	Ps. 106:1-12
12-Jul	1 Chron. 11:10-12:40	Acts 16:1-15	Ps. 106:13-27
13-Jul	1 Chron. 13-15	Acts 16:16-40	Ps. 106:28-33
14-Jul	1 Chron. 16-17	Acts 17:1-14	Ps. 106:34-43
15-Jul	1 Chron. 18-20	Acts 17:15-34	Ps. 106:44-48
16-Jul	1 Chron. 21-22	Acts 18:1-23	Ps. 107:1-9
17-Jul	1 Chron. 23-25	Acts 18:24-19:10	Ps. 107:10-16
18-Jul	1 Chron. 26-27	Acts 19:11-22	Ps. 107:17-32
19-Jul	1 Chron. 28-29	Acts 19:23-41	Ps. 107:33-38
20-Jul	2 Chron. 1-3	Acts 20:1-16	Ps. 107:39-43
21-Jul	2 Chron. 4:1-6:11	Acts 20:17-38	Ps. 108
22-Jul	2 Chron. 6:12-7:10	Acts 21:1-14	Ps. 109:1-20
23-Jul	2 Chron. 7:11-9:28	Acts 21:15-32	Ps. 109:21-31
24-Jul	2 Chron. 9:29-12:16	Acts 21:33-22:16	Ps. 110:1-3
25-Jul	2 Chron. 13-15	Acts 22:17-23:11	Ps. 110:4-7
26-Jul	2 Chron. 16-17	Acts 23:12-24:21	Ps. 111
27-Jul	2 Chron. 18-19	Acts 24:22-25:12	Ps. 112
28-Jul	2 Chron. 20-21	Acts 25:13-27	Ps. 113
29-Jul	2 Chron. 22-23	Acts 26	Ps. 114
30-Jul	2 Chron. 24:1-25:16	Acts 27:1-20	Ps. 115:1-10
31-Jul	2 Chron. 25:17-27:9	Acts 27:21-28:6	Ps. 115:11-18
1-Aug	2 Chron. 28:1-29:19	Acts 28:7-31	Ps. 116:1-5
2-Aug	2 Chron. 29:20-30:27	Rom. 1:1-17	Ps. 116:6-19

3-Aug	2 Chron. 31-32	Rom. 1:18-32	Ps. 117
4-Aug	2 Chron. 33:1-34:7	Rom. 2	Ps. 118:1-18
5-Aug	2 Chron. 34:8-35:19	Rom. 3:1-26	Ps. 118:19-23
6-Aug	2 Chron. 35:20-36:23	Rom. 3:27-4:25	Ps. 118:24-29
7-Aug	Ezra 1-3	Rom. 5	Ps. 119:1-8
8-Aug	Ezra 4-5	Rom. 6:1-7:6	Ps. 119:9-16
9-Aug	Ezra 6:1-7:26	Rom. 7:7-25	Ps. 119:17-32
10-Aug	Ezra 7:27-9:4	Rom. 8:1-27	Ps. 119:33-40
11-Aug	Ezra 9:5-10:44	Rom. 8:28-39	Ps. 119:41-64
12-Aug	Neh. 1:1-3:16	Rom. 9:1-18	Ps. 119:65-72
13-Aug	Neh. 3:17-5:13	Rom. 9:19-33	Ps. 119:73-80
14-Aug	Neh. 5:14-7:73	Rom. 10:1-13	Ps. 119:81-88
15-Aug	Neh. 8:1-9:5	Rom. 10:14-11:24	Ps. 119:89-104
16-Aug	Neh. 9:6-10:27	Rom. 11:25-12:8	Ps. 119:105-120
17-Aug	Neh. 10:28-12:26	Rom. 12:9-13:7	Ps. 119:121-128
18-Aug	Neh. 12:27-13:31	Rom. 13:8-14:12	Ps. 119:129-136
19-Aug	Esther 1:1-2:18	Rom. 14:13-15:13	Ps. 119:137-152
20-Aug	Esther 2:19-5:14	Rom. 15:14-21	Ps. 119:153-168
21-Aug	Esther. 6-8	Rom. 15:22-33	Ps. 119:169-176
22-Aug	Esther 9-10	Rom. 16	Ps. 120-122
23-Aug	Job 1-3	1 Cor. 1:1-25	Ps. 123
24-Aug	Job 4-6	1 Cor. 1:26-2:16	Ps. 124-125
25-Aug	Job 7-9	1 Cor. 3	Ps. 126-127
26-Aug	Job 10-13	1 Cor. 4:1-13	Ps. 128-129
27-Aug	Job 14-16	1 Cor. 4:14-5:13	Ps. 130
28-Aug	Job 17-20	1 Cor. 6	Ps. 131
29-Aug	Job 21-23	1 Cor. 7:1-16	Ps. 132
30-Aug	Job 24-27	1 Cor. 7:17-40	Ps. 133-134
31-Aug	Job 28-30	1 Cor. 8	Ps. 135
1-Sep	Job 31-33	1 Cor. 9:1-18	Ps. 136:1-9
2-Sep	Job 34-36	1 Cor. 9:19-10:13	Ps. 136:10-26
3-Sep	Job 37-39	1 Cor. 10:14-11:1	Ps. 137
4-Sep	Job 40-42	1 Cor. 11:2-34	Ps. 138
5-Sep	Eccles. 1:1-3:15	1 Cor. 12:1-26	Ps. 139:1-6
6-Sep	Eccles. 3:16-6:12	1 Cor. 12:27-13:13	Ps. 139:7-18
7-Sep	Eccles. 7:1-9:12	1 Cor. 14:1-22	Ps. 139:19-24

8-Sep	Eccles. 9:13-12:14	1 Cor. 14:23-15:11	Ps. 140:1-8
9-Sep	SS 1-4	1 Cor. 15:12-34	Ps. 140:9-13
10-Sep	SS 5-8	1 Cor. 15:35-58	Ps. 141
11-Sep	Isa. 1-2	1 Cor. 16	Ps. 142
12-Sep	Isa. 3-5	2 Cor. 1:1-11	Ps. 143:1-6
13-Sep	Isa. 6-8	2 Cor. 1:12-2:4	Ps. 143:7-12
14-Sep	Isa. 9-10	2 Cor. 2:5-17	Ps. 144
15-Sep	Isa. 11-13	2 Cor. 3	Ps. 145
16-Sep	Isa. 14-16	2 Cor. 4	Ps. 146
17-Sep	Isa. 17-19	2 Cor. 5	Ps. 147:1-11
18-Sep	Isa. 20-23	2 Cor. 6	Ps. 147:12-20
19-Sep	Isa. 24:1-26:19	2 Cor. 7	Ps. 148
20-Sep	Isa. 26:20-28:29	2 Cor. 8	Ps. 149-150
21-Sep	Isa. 29-30	2 Cor. 9	Prov. 1:1-9
22-Sep	Isa. 31-33	2 Cor. 10	Prov. 1:10-22
23-Sep	Isa. 34-36	2 Cor. 11	Prov. 1:23-26
24-Sep	Isa. 37-38	2 Cor. 12:1-10	Prov. 1:27-33
25-Sep	Isa. 39-40	2 Cor. 12:11-13:14	Prov. 2:1-15
26-Sep	Isa. 41-42	Gal. 1	Prov. 2:16-22
27-Sep	Isa. 43:1-44:20	Gal. 2	Prov. 3:1-12
28-Sep	Isa. 44:21-46:13	Gal. 3:1-18	Prov. 3:13-26
29-Sep	Isa. 47:1-49:13	Gal 3:19-29	Prov. 3:27-35
30-Sep	Isa. 49:14-51:23	Gal 4:1-11	Prov. 4:1-19
1-Oct	Isa. 52-54	Gal. 4:12-31	Prov. 4:20-27
2-Oct	Isa. 55-57	Gal. 5	Prov. 5:1-14
3-Oct	Isa. 58-59	Gal. 6	Prov. 5:15-23
4-Oct	Isa. 60-62	Eph. 1	Prov. 6:1-5
5-Oct	Isa. 63:1-65:16	Eph. 2	Prov. 6:6-19
6-Oct	Isa. 65:17-66:24	Eph. 3:1-4:16	Prov. 6:20-26
7-Oct	Jer. 1-2	Eph. 4:17-32	Prov. 6:27-35
8-Oct	Jer. 3:1-4:22	Eph. 5	Prov. 7:1-5
9-Oct	Jer. 4:23-5:31	Eph. 6	Prov. 7:6-27
10-Oct	Jer. 6:1-7:26	Phil. 1:1-26	Prov. 8:1-11
11-Oct	Jer. 7:26-9:16	Phil. 1:27-2:18	Prov. 8:12-21
12-Oct	Jer. 9:17-11:17	Phil 2:19-30	Prov. 8:22-36
13-Oct	Jer. 11:18-13:27	Phil. 3	Prov. 9:1-6

19-Nov	Ezek. 24-26	Heb. 11:32-40	Prov. 19:15-21
20-Nov	Ezek. 27-28	Heb. 12:1-13	Prov. 19:22-29
21-Nov	Ezek. 29-30	Heb. 12:14-29	Prov. 20:1-18
22-Nov	Ezek. 31-32	Heb. 13	Prov. 20:19-24
23-Nov	Ezek. 33:1-34:10	Jas. 1	Prov. 20:25-30
24-Nov	Ezek. 34:11-36:15	Jas. 2	Prov. 21:1-8
25-Nov	Ezek. 36:16-37:28	Jas. 3	Prov. 21:9-18
26-Nov	Ezek. 38-39	Jas. 4:1-5:6	Prov. 21:19-24
27-Nov	Ezek. 40	Jas. 5:7-20	Prov. 21:25-31
28-Nov	Ezek. 41:1-43:12	1 Pet. 1:1-12	Prov. 22:1-9
29-Nov	Ezek. 43:13-44:31	1 Pet. 1:13-2:3	Prov. 22:10-23
30-Nov	Ezek. 45-46	1 Pet. 2:4-17	Prov. 22:24-29
1-Dec	Ezek. 47-48	1 Pet. 2:18-3:7	Prov. 23:1-9
2-Dec	Dan. 1:1-2:23	1 Pet. 3:8-4:19	Prov. 23:10-16
3-Dec	Dan. 2:24-3:30	1 Pet. 5	Prov. 23:17-25
4-Dec	Dan. 4	2 Pet. 1	Prov. 23:26-35
5-Dec	Dan. 5	2 Pet. 2	Prov. 24:1-18
6-Dec	Dan. 6:1-7:14	2 Pet. 3	Prov. 24:19-27
7-Dec	Dan. 7:15-8:27	1 John 1:1-2:17	Prov. 24:28-34
8-Dec	Dan. 9-10	1 John 2:18-29	Prov. 25:1-12
9-Dec	Dan. 11-12	1 John 3:1-12	Prov. 25:13-17
10-Dec	Hos. 1-3	1 John 3:13-4:16	Prov. 25:18-28
11-Dec	Hos. 4-6	1 John 4:17-5:21	Prov. 26:1-16
12-Dec	Hos. 7-10	2 John	Prov. 26:17-21
13-Dec	Hos. 11-14	3 John	Prov. 26:22-27:9
14-Dec	Joel 1:1-2:17	Jude	Prov. 27:10-17
15-Dec	Joel 2:18-3:21	Rev. 1:1-2:11	Prov. 27:18-27
16-Dec	Amos 1:1-4:5	Rev. 2:12-29	Prov. 28:1-8
17-Dec	Amos 4:6-6:14	Rev. 3	Prov. 28:9-16
18-Dec	Amos 7-9	Rev. 4:1-5:5	Prov. 28:17-24
19-Dec	Obad-Jonah	Rev. 5:6-14	Prov. 28:25-28
20-Dec	Mic. 1:1-4:5	Rev. 6:1-7:8	Prov. 29:1-8
21-Dec	Mic. 4:6-7:20	Rev. 7:9-8:13	Prov. 29:9-14
22-Dec	Nah. 1-3	Rev. 9-10	Prov. 29:15-23
23-Dec	Hab. 1-3	Rev. 11	Prov. 29:24-27
24-Dec	Zeph. 1-3	Rev. 12	Prov. 30:1-6

25-DEC	HAG. 1-2	REV. 13:1-14:13	PROV. 30:7-16
26-DEC	ZECH. 1-4	REV. 14:14-16:3	PROV. 30:17-20
27-DEC	ZECH. 5-8	REV. 16:4-21	PROV. 30:21-28
28-DEC	ZECH. 9-11	REV. 17:1-18:8	PROV. 30:29-33
29-DEC	ZECH. 12-14	REV. 18:9-24	PROV. 31:1-9
30-DEC	MAL. 1-2	REV. 19-20	PROV. 31:10-17
31-DEC	MAL. 3-4	REV. 21-22	PROV. 31:18-31

Expanded Editions of
The Bible Promise Book® Just for Women

The Bible Promise Book® for Morning & Evening Women's Edition

The Bible Promise Book® is now available in a *Morning & Evening* edition for women, featuring an inspiring promise book theme twice a day for every day of the year. With Bible promises arranged into morning and evening readings—including God's Word, Wisdom, Faith, Prayer, Encouragement, Love, Joy, and more—each scripture speaks directly to the heart, drawing readers ever closer to their heavenly Father.

DiCarta / 978-1-63409-708-6 / $16.99

Everyday Bible Promises for Women Journal

Barbour's Bible Promise Books® are perennial best-sellers, with millions of copies sold. Here's a fantastic journal just for women, featuring an inspiring scriptural theme for every day of the year. Covering topics like Wisdom, Faith, Prayer, Encouragement, Love, Joy, and more—each scripture will speak directly to your heart, drawing you ever closer to your heavenly Father.

Hardback / 978-1-68322-344-3 / $19.99